THE DESCENT
OF MIND

THE DESCENT OF MIND

The Nature and Purpose of Intelligence

Peter Evans
and
Geoff Deehan

GRAFTON BOOKS

A Division of the Collins Publishing Group

LONDON GLASGOW
TORONTO SYDNEY AUCKLAND

Grafton Books
A Division of the Collins Publishing Group
8 Grafton Street, London W1X 3LA

Published by Grafton Books 1990

British Library Cataloguing in Publication Data

Evans, Peter
The descent of mind: the nature and purpose of intelligence
1. Man. Intelligence
I. Title   II. Deehan, Geoff
153.9

ISBN 0-246-13275-2

Photoset by Rowland Phototypesetting Limited
Bury St Edmunds, Suffolk
Printed in Great Britain by
William Collins Sons & Co. Ltd, Glasgow

For Charles

CONTENTS

PREFACE

This is a book about intelligence. Whatever that is. When people are asked 'What is intelligence?' they tend to reply: 'I don't know how to define it, but I can certainly recognize it when I see it.' Actually, what they often mean is that the people they find 'intelligent' are those whose minds work very like their own; they agree with an opinion or share a common purpose. The political ally is intelligent, as is the employer who sees your worth or the teacher who endorses your essay. Intelligence here is less something that you see in others than a quality projected from yourself.

That in itself is odd. Surely a mental ability or a way of grappling with problems, or however else you encapsulate the word 'intelligence', either exists or does not? Whatever the observer thinks and feels is surely irrelevant? In fact, as we shall see in the course of this book, intelligence is not just one, unitary, intellectual feature. And it does very much vary from one observer to another: like beauty, it rests in the eye of the beholder.

One of the difficulties of tackling a subject such as intelligence is that here is a word in very common, everyday use, with hundreds of local definitions. So should we begin by defining our terms and stating at the outset what it is we are talking about? Perhaps we should. However, according to Professor Marvin Minsky from the Massachusetts Institute of Technology: 'There's no reason to think that "intelligence" does have any particularly sharp meaning. It's a very large and messy network of many different ideas. So when we say we are studying intelligence we mean that we're trying to understand the kinds of phenomena that are tied loosely to that word. It wouldn't do any good to try to define it.'

The point is well made but, in a way, this whole book is an attempt to unravel or, at least, describe that 'messy network' of ideas that constitutes intelligence. And in that attempt we have been aided by some of the ablest thinkers today engaged in trying to understand the true nature of this much-vaunted and controversial quality of mind. For their intelligence, many thanks.

1

IN THE EYE OF THE BEHOLDER

There is a small but dedicated fraternity of radio astronomers convinced of the value of a project known as 'SETI' – the Search for Extra Terrestrial Intelligence. They hope, some of them even expect, that eventually they will find, among the teeming millions of stars, a sign of life elsewhere in the universe. They have no idea what manner of creature will provide this evidence that we are not alone in space. All they do know is that it will share with humans a quality that enables us to use technology to transmit information across hundreds, thousands, even millions of light years. That quality, of course, is 'intelligence'. Actually, the SETI buffs expect any messages to come from organisms that are 'super-intelligent'. They reason that if other civilizations have evolved into an age of high technology they are, statistically speaking, unlikely still to be at the fumbling, infantile stages that we are going through on Earth. If they know about nuclear energy, electronics, biotechnology or space vehicles, they probably have done so not for decades like us, but perhaps for thousands of years. They may, of course, be virtually on an intellectual par with humankind. But that would be too much of a coincidence. No. If there is intelligence out there, it will be advanced, superior, and humbling in its sheer power.

While we speculate, as many a science fiction writer has done, on what impact the loss of our cosmic isolation might have, we might dwell too on what we mean by an extraterrestrial 'intelligence'. And the more we do so, the more we realize what we cannot say with any certainty about the nature of this alien intelligence. It would, for example, be rash to assume that our intergalactic pen-pals are even 'conscious beings, like us'. Biologically of course they may be nothing at all like us; their bodies could be put together with an altogether different sort of biochemistry, based on silicon, say, not carbon. As to what they might look like, anyone's guess is as good as anyone else's. More to the point though, these extraterrestrials may not be 'beings' with 'consciousness' as we understand those terms at all.

Imagine this scenario. The distant planet from which messages emanate had, a few million years ago, reached a level of technological sophistication similar to that of Earth a few decades from today. The computer scientists on Planet X have managed to build machines that are programmed to make improved copies of themselves. They are self-replicating, 'evolving' computers, passing on knowledge and skills from one generation to the next. Now suppose that their living creators and all others of the species were totally wiped out by a devastating virus, leaving behind their tireless computers which are becoming more and more clever with each passing generation. Before the extraterrestrials perished, they too had in progress a SETI programme. They had set their supercomputers the problem of finding an effective means of making extra-galactic contact. Eventually the progressively cleverer machines come up with a solution which works. They successfully beam a message to us. Thus the 'extraterrestrial intelligence' we believe we have detected is in reality just these very machines finding a way to catch our attention. Is a message pumped out tirelessly by a computer network truly the artefact of an 'intelligence'?

The computers cannot be said to be 'conscious' of what they are doing, any more than a dishwasher is conscious of continually passing through its wash/rinse/dry cycles or a traffic light of changing colours to direct motorists. On the other hand, does a machine necessarily have to be conscious or self-aware in order to behave intelligently?

No doubt, if the SETI project ever manages to realize its ambition, psychologists, philosophers, experts in artificial intelligence, neuroscientists and lay observers will debate that long-standing question with renewed eagerness. Meanwhile it remains one of the enigmas surrounding our frequent, if loose, deployment of this term 'intelligence'. There are many other issues arising from the same word. Most if not all of them will be aired in the course of this book.

Why intelligence?

A second theme we shall be investigating, for example, relates to the first. It concerns not just the presence or absence of intelligence but the need for this capacity in the first place. Why should human beings have evolved into intelligent creatures? Presumably we have done so because such a feature is adaptive: it fits us better for our environment, in the same way as echolocation serves the bat hunting for prey in the dark or inbuilt bio-compasses the much-travelled pigeon or the bee.

Yet it might be argued that intelligence could be more of a liability than a benefit. We may have evolved into animals competently equipped to ensure our self-destruction. Where would be the 'evolutionary advantage' in being set on a nuclear kamikaze mission? Bear in mind too that intelligence – or at least the higher order intelligence we associate with humankind – is not necessary for success in evolutionary terms. The small-brained dinosaurs, so often erroneously regarded as unsuccessful because they ultimately perished in an Armageddon of unknown cause, flourished for approximately 60 million years. Our species has only been around for a small fraction of that time, say 4½ million years. Only when we have stayed the course for another 50 million years or so can we congratulate ourselves on being the smartest animals in creation.

What is intelligence?

It seems, on the face of it, an unnecessary question. But it is not. An analogy will serve to illustrate the point. In the curious, Alice-in-Wonderland domain of sub-atomic particle physics, researchers have in recent years come across some mysterious phenomena. Perhaps the most bizarre of all are what are known as 'observer-dependent' effects. Light can take two forms: waves, analogous to radio waves; and quanta, or discrete 'packets' of energy. Experiments have shown that the form light takes seems dependent not, as one might think, on objective factors such as environmental conditions, but on how the experimenter chooses to look at it. In fact, even more strange, it seems as if the switch from quantum to wave can take place *retroactively*: the observer can, to all intents and purposes, reverse the arrow of time to influence events in the past.

In other words, light is not one thing but two. What you see depends on your viewpoint. Something similar may be said of intelligence, except that this time it is not a question of a two-sided phenomenon but of many sides, each showing its particular face according to who is looking. And how. If you are a schoolteacher, intelligence might be the quality of mind that marks out one pupil from another. It is here comparable to, say, 'athletic prowess' that makes some people run, jump or swim better than others. On the other hand, a biologist would tend to see intelligence not so much as the key to achievement as a route to survival: intelligence here is the power to adapt to change, threat and the unexpected. All human beings possess this skill. Indeed that is how and why they have survived in the evolutionary struggle. We are, according to this criterion, all winners.

In addition, what kind of intelligence – and there is surely more than one kind – you observe depends on where you look for it. One place might be a university or a law court, where college graduates with elevated professional qualifications hold sway. But this is not the only place. Far from it.

Phil: a study in fluency
It is a hot summer afternoon. A busy street-market is in full swing. Fruit and vegetables cover the stalls; so too does every other imaginable household product, from baby clothes to plastic buckets, aftershave to video cassettes. A large, happy crowd has a superabundance of consumer goods on which to spend its money. The stallholders too are in fine form, each delivering the rapid, carefully-designed sales pitch that means the difference between a transaction made and a potential customer lost in the crowd. Of all these appeals to consumerism, one in particular stands out from the rest. From behind a stall laden with unopened boxes and un-marked packages an 'auctioneer' has an enthralled audience of perhaps 40 people. Phil has been in this business for 15 years, and he is acknowledged by his fellow-traders as a craftsman of rare skill. His basic strategy is simple. From out of his audience he will try to hook eight individuals – 'eight lucky people only, sorry, just eight' – and keep them in his verbal thrall until he has relieved them of a substantial sum of money as they progressively 'invest' in more and more of his goods.

Phil is a humorous, fast-talking 'spieler' with a fantasti-cally well-attuned eye for a prospective 'mark'. He is aided by a few associates planted in the crowd who periodically 'Ooh' and 'Ah' at Phil's offers and themselves rush forward with wads of banknotes to be the beneficiaries of this self-sacrificial mock auction. The eight marks are initially brought on board by an age-old ploy: 'Who'll give me one pound for what's in this box? Just one pound?' As the hands go up, Phil leaps in with 'Here, not just this box but this one as well.' More confident now, the eight speculators have identified themselves.

Phil then executes a breathtaking manoeuvre. He opens the two boxes in which are some quite good-looking items; in one a gold-coloured necklace on a black satin backing, in the other box a colourful porcelain shepherdess. As the crowd is appreciating the value for money, Phil in a spasm of altruism says to the expectant eight: 'Just to show you that I appreciate a lively punter, I won't even take your money. Have these lovely items free of charge.' The crowd gasps and Phil carefully lays out a row of eight boxes, then another on top. Next comes the crucial step. 'Now,' he says to the eight, 'you know I'm a bit of a sport. How would you like to take another chance and offer me five pounds for this?' So saying he takes from under the stall another, much bigger box and puts it on the table. He arranges this box with the other two so that they form a large pile. 'All this,' says Phil with a broad flourish, 'for a fiver.' If there is any hesitation, Phil's associates deaden it with grunts of approval and encouragement. The eight pay over their £5. They are, now, conclusively and inexorably on a ladder that will take them up – or is it down? – to an outlay of at least £50 and will net them a lot of fairly trashy, if light-catching, items that they would almost certainly not have bought under normal circumstances. But circumstances here are far from normal. Phil sees to that.

He possesses an extraordinary range of aptitudes and skills. Verbally proficient, with an inexhaustible flow of interesting and amusing patter, he has a profound insight into the psychology of others which he exploits and manipulates to his own ends. The way he structures his sales pitch is nothing short of masterly. He plays on the moods and feelings of his enthralled audiences like a virtuoso violinist coaxing undreamed-of depths from a Stradivarius. A simplistic description of Phil is that he is 'streetwise', a product of the rough and tumble of his difficult business. But that term covers a multitude of behaviours that, in another context, we would deem highly 'intelligent'.

Imagine, for example, not a street market but a political debating chamber such as the House of Commons or the

US Senate. People like Phil with something to sell (not cheap jewellery and china but budgets and policies) are constantly on their feet using a sales pitch – here known as 'oratory' – in much the same way as the market trader. There are 'plants' in the audience too, in the shape of followers from the same party, and a certain amount of subterfuge in presenting the message in the best light. The packaging here is purely verbal. Tax increases are 'necessary revenue-raising measures', a continuing war in a remote country is 'part of our long-term plan for peace' and so on.

One is tempted to speculate how well people like Phil would fare in this arena. However, that must remain merely speculation because Phil was a complete dud at school, leaving early and starting work with no examination certificates or other qualifications. His political analogues are pretty well all cast from a different mould: good education; good qualifications; sound careers and so on. Thus, from one perspective, they are quite dissimilar. In the way that the world at large judges and categorizes people, the politician belongs to the highly educated 'intelligent' group, while Phil does not. In terms of what intellectual gifts each possesses, they are remarkably alike. Indeed, Phil may even have the edge, because few politicians manage to peddle their wares so successfully for as long as he has.

Undeniably, we often fall into the trap of classifying people as more or less 'intelligent' when we really mean that they have a better or worse paid job or move in circles deemed to be of greater or lesser social or intellectual clout. The successful professional criminal, for example, who enjoys a reasonable standard of living by periodically relieving banks of the contents of their strongboxes, would hardly ever be thought of in the same context as, say, the university lecturer in palaeoanthropology or the computer systems analyst. Again, though, the distinction is not so much one of mental capacities as of demonstrable achievement within a framework of social convention.

To be a university type is to have a 'better job'. To become a top computer man is to have passed a lot of exams. To be a bank robber is to be looked down on as disreputable. There are, moreover, no paper qualifications needed for doing the job. It is outside the social frame. However, it still exists as a profession and some people do it a lot better than others. They are the clever ones. And their cleverness is no different from that of any other professional.

Essential intelligence

To understand 'intelligence' or 'intelligent behaviour' or whatever phrase you care to choose to describe what George Santayana called 'quickness in seeing things as they are', one has to divorce it from its social context. This is now recognized as the only way to get to the heart of the matter. But it was not always so, as certain would-be recruits to the US Army discovered during World War One. They were given a number of tests to determine suitability, including one question on whether the nickname for the Brooklyn Nationals was 'The Giants', 'The Orioles', 'The Superbas' or 'The Indians'. For the All-American Boy whose teenage years had been spent following favourite teams and reading the sports pages, such questions were quickly dealt with. For the Italian or Jewish immigrant, living in what was still a foreign environment, cocooned within a native culture, American baseball would be as much of a mystery as cricket is even now to most of the world. They failed the tests on the grounds of inferior innate mental ability. Cultural bias can operate at any level of test or problem. Consider this example.

Why are Geography, Drama, Art and English in the ascendant? It would be well-nigh impossible to come up with an answer to that riddle unless you were locked in closely to a particular culture. It is unlikely, for example, that you could begin to find a solution unless you knew something about Western music. A correct answer is most likely to come from one of that fairly limited number of people who learn to play a musical instrument. In particular you would need to be (or have been) a violinist to spot that the initial letters of Geography, Drama, Art and English name the violin's strings from the lowest upwards.

There is considerable culture-rich knowledge packed into this problem, without which one is severely handicapped in trying to resolve it. Of course a certain cleverness is required to 'read' the question, to crack the setter's code. But this is something that comes with practice: one can acquire the turn of mind needed to get on the right track. What really makes this and similar problems difficult is its cultural component.

The story of the attempt to measure that evocative quality we call intelligence – be it wholly inborn and determined by our genetic endowment or shaped in large measure by the environments in which we are raised – is a catalogue of maladroitness on the part of the measurers. Sometimes the testers began from a position of what we would now call prejudice; sometimes they were unclear as to what they were testing; sometimes there was good old-fashioned chicanery going on. This is not to say that 'tests of intelligence' on the whole are worthless. They do have some value in certain well-defined contexts. But it is to remind anyone who believes that human mental capacity can be put to the tape measure, like a neck or chest circumference, that such methods have their limitations.

Unfortunately, though, many people do still subscribe to the psychometric notion, and use it to construct not just a mental hierarchy but a socio-political one.

Intellectual power politics

Intelligence is a political hot potato and has been ever since the early days of psychometric testing. By attaching to individuals a label in the form of a firm number or score, we are already establishing a social hierarchy. If, in addition, it is argued that such a score is predominantly a function of one's genetic endowment, and thus by implication relatively immutable, then we have the basis of a legitimized discriminatory system, with the 'best brains' at the top and the inferior mortals below. In short, intelligence can be central to a modern form of eugenics, that infamous, pseudo-scientific philosophy that reached its nadir with Hitler's racial policies in the thirties and forties. So too today. If, say, a person of Afro-Caribbean stock takes an IQ test, his or her score can, if one so chooses, be treated as some index of inherent racial 'quality'.

In other words, intelligence testing can be used to demonstrate that blacks are inferior to whites. We shall be looking in detail at this alleged 'inferiority' later in this book. As it happens the issue is rather more complicated, if not paradoxical, than both sides in the debate over the genetic basis of racial differences in intelligence tend to admit.

For one thing, even if it were true that one racial type or ethnic group did score higher or lower than the next, what then? We shall be seeing later how flexible IQ scores can be within the space of a single generation, and that environmental factors can produce gigantic increases from whatever baseline. Secondly, the tests themselves are only a limited measure of intelligence. According to the psychologist Leon Kamin, to regard 'IQ tests as measures of "intelligence" is nonsensical'. And as Sir Walter Bodmer remarks, 'Intelligence must not be confused with IQ as measured by an IQ test.' Even Cyril Burt, a guru of selection by psychometric testing, believed that 'Tests . . . can be but the beginning, never the end, of the examination of the child.' Another theme we shall be exploring in this book is how much there is to intelligence beyond the confines of the conventional test.

Seeing the light

What goes on in the head of the clever person? How does the intelligent mind machine really work? Comic strip artists and cartoonists are inordinately fond of representing a sudden idea by a balloon with a light bulb shining within. Indeed, the language of intelligence is light-intensive. An idea 'dawns'. It is 'bright' – as is the person who gets it. A scientific theory 'sheds light' on an interesting but murky body of data, while the thoughts of a Shakespeare or a Dante provide 'illuminating' insights into the condition and destiny of humanity.

This notion of intelligence as radiant force has an early echo in the Bible: 'Let there be light' is both a literal and a metaphorical exhortation. God brings to the darkness of the world he has just created the guiding, directive light of his Supreme Intelligence. Louis XIV – the Sun King – was similarly the ultimate source of secular wisdom by personifying the most powerful light in the heavens. That great upsurge in intellectual ferment was the Enlightenment, while, throughout history, human beings have been thrilled and excited by 'flashes of inspiration'.

To 'see the light', though, is in a way a strange metaphor for intelligent activity. It gives the impression that having ideas is akin to switching on a lamp in a darkened room, making a sudden, dramatic impact on a sombre or confused state. However, most of the time thinking or behaving intelligently is more like gradually seeing in the dark when the lights are still *off*. At first there is blackness. But then the eye begins dimly to perceive one or two features, then distances and relationships are established, until an incomplete but tolerably coherent picture of the environment emerges.

It is often thus with 'bright ideas'. For every anecdote such as that related by Kekulé, who professed to have discovered the ring structure of the benzene molecule through an illuminating insight provided by a dream of a snake biting its own tail, there is a more low-key or incremental account of a discovery or creative achievement: Beethoven toiling away at version after version of his musical compositions; the novelist Flaubert painstakingly fitting words together like a mosaic craftsman; Darwin eventually putting together his evolutionary theories after years of study and observation in the field.

For the first time in the history of brain research it is now becoming possible to reconcile the genesis and development of ideas with the neural machinery that makes them possible, to see, albeit imperfectly at present, what goes on in the thinking brain. Later in the book we will look at intelligent behaviour in some of its many forms and how this can be squared with what is known about the grey matter that produces it.

Intelligent living

A constant feature of what we term 'intelligent behaviour' in the broadest sense – which takes in just about any sort of human behaviour you can imagine – is its variation within and between individuals. This is not just a matter of one person's IQ score being higher than another's. Nor is it the difference between academic achievements, professional status or general renown. It is rather the frequently observed fact that some very bright people act the part in some circumstances but can be woefully stupid in others.

Take the case of Fiona and Antonia, two school friends

and now college graduates, both with good degrees in the Humanities and pretty well matched for intellectual endowment. They are different, though, in many other respects. Antonia is alert, down-to-earth, a little dour and unwilling to suffer fools gladly, where Fiona is less focused, charming, more sympathetic towards the failings of others and always in demand at parties. At nineteen they both fell in love, with different men, and the progress of these first, major affairs reveals some startling differences in 'intelligence'. When Fiona announced to her parents that this was 'It – the Real Thing' they groaned. She was only in her second year at university and having to work fairly hard to keep up with the demands of her course. Their experience of Fiona's earlier juvenile romances suggested to them that she could quite easily waste her whole future by getting too involved with this undeniably attractive partner. To their surprise, though, the often vacant, disorganized, apparently easily-led Fiona started to timetable her life in an unprecedented fashion. She set aside times for work and time for boyfriend. She maintained her usual wide circle of social contacts, of both sexes, and seemed to be not so much led off target by her new-found love as revitalized by it. Taking her degree without too much difficulty, she went off into a smiling future. She did not, incidentally, marry and live happily ever after with her 'real thing', but that is another story.

With Antonia quite the opposite happened. The usually self - disciplined - to - the - point - of - imitating - a - railway - timetable mentality simply evaporated in a cloud of amorous euphoria. College studies went into the doldrums; she saw hardly anything of her former friends; and spent an intense year or so staring into her lover's eyes. She ran into a lot of trouble with the academic authorities at the university, re-sitting exams and only just managing to scrape a Final degree by a combination of good fortune and applied panic. She too did not settle down with her beloved. In fact they parted company before the final degree ceremony. And she left university feeling that she had somehow missed out on what it had to offer.

Both in the way they behave compared to each other and in their apparent lack of internal consistency, you could say that Fiona and Antonia are displaying considerable differences in intelligence. They are not alone. As a political strategist Adolf Hitler was undoubtedly a genius. The way in which he skilfully appealed to various sectors of German society to gain power and promote National Socialism was a masterly demonstration of manipulative skill by a grandmaster of politics. Yet Hitler ultimately behaved in a stupid manner demonstrated by some major strategic blunders. So too did Napoleon whose Great Army was also sacrificed on the altar of folly in the disastrous Russian campaign. So often, within a single individual, co-exist two intelligences, one high and one low: the brilliant professor of physics who is incapable of fixing a broken fuse; the lofty philosophical thinker who cannot answer 'yes' or 'no' to the most mundane question; the decisive military man of action who has not a clue as to how to discipline his own children.

Clever animals = intelligent animals?

Some idea of the complexity of the concept of intelligence can be gleaned from what one might term the Cleverness/ Intelligence Threshold – CIT. CIT is that point at which behaviour that is merely slick or well-trained and even 'mindless' ends and what most of us might call 'intelligent' begins. We can see the difficulties of drawing the CIT dividing line if we consider a few examples drawn from ethology – the study of animal behaviour.

It has become fashionable to call the dolphin 'intelligent'. Here is an aquatic mammal with an unusually large brain, a complex click-whistle language and an endearing affinity with humans. Dolphins can quite quickly learn a variety of tasks and tricks, and seem capable of a human-like purposefulness and even a sense of humour. It is unsurprising, therefore, that we think of them as being close to us on the broad tree of intelligence. Few of us would have the same feelings of rapport with, say, a pigeon or an ant, yet here too one observes some apparently very intelligent behaviour. A pigeon, for example, is an excellent navigator, with several inbuilt homing mechanisms including a biological compass. It also has a remarkable ability to recognize objects when it can see only a part of the overall image. Admittedly this is a task that a three-year-old child can accomplish with ease. At the same time, many excellent minds have been applied to solving precisely this problem using a computer.

No machine yet exists with anything approaching the pigeon's pattern recognition facility. All the resources of the world's great universities and research centres have not equalled the bird-brained pigeon. Think too of the common garden ant. Watch a colony in action and ask yourself whether any human society comes as close in organizational expertise and social cohesion. There is superb division of labour, self-sacrifice and a fundamental 'socialist' spirit that puts the fruits of the Russian Revolution to shame. There, in short, is a model sharing society. Now the ant, like the pigeon, is a relatively small-brained creature. It is not like the dolphin or the chimpanzee in showing some kind of relationship with human beings. Yet its behaviour is remarkable for its complexity, discipline and sophistication. Are we really sure that we can draw a CIT line between this and the tricks of the dolphin or sealion?

Consider now lions on the hunt. A group of lionesses has been observed to 'plan' a hunting party like generals huddled around a battlefield map. They group together, then disperse to various parts of the plain, one animal on high ground –

directing operations, perhaps – one crouched hidden, another rushing at a prey to send it into the jaws of the waiting lioness. Not only is this co-operation on the hunt. It also implies that lions possess a mental quality usually thought to be unique to humans – the ability to think in the abstract about the future: 'If we do this, then that should happen', and so on. Again, lions make uncomfortable intellectual bedfellows. We might well concede that chimpanzees can, in a limited way, handle abstract concepts, but lions? Could it be that lions too can hold in their minds a concept of the future?

As a general rule the more we look at other species the cleverer they seem to become. The bee communicates the direction of a food source through its remarkable 'waggle dance'; the female plover feigns a broken wing to distract a predator that might swoop on her young; the monkey gives evidence of a rudimentary skill in arithmetic. It may be that, in all the cases, animals are behaving as the mindless products of their evolutionary history, as automata driven by the relentless force of instinct. Certainly it would be rash to interpret every sign of human-like cleverness as indicative of human-like intelligence. That would be anthropomorphism of a most misguided sort.

On the other hand, many ethologists are beginning to revise their views about where the CIT now lies in a number of species. They are beginning to wonder not so much whether other animals are intelligent, but what experiments or investigations they might carry out to prove that they are. It is the researchers themselves who need to demonstrate their intelligence now.

Not only is there a hazy boundary separating 'cleverness' and 'intelligence' in animals: there is a CIT with humans as well. The practised skill of a fisherman twisting a heavy rope into a secure knot to moor his boat; the kaleidoscopic *tour de force* of the circus juggler, spinning an impossible number of objects between his hands; the deft economy of movement of an assembly-line worker in an electronics factory, nimble fingers putting together printed circuit boards – again we have to ask ourselves whether these are what it is to be intelligent, or whether such manual skills are simply conditioned responses, nothing more than elaborately and painstakingly trained reflexes in action. We shall be delving deeper into that question, too, a little later.

The first question we need to address, however, is the one we posed at the very outset. What is this thing called 'intelligence'?

2

INTELLIGENT BEHAVIOUR

In the beginning was 'g', the idea that there is some single, unifying quality that we can call intelligence. That we can test and assess it, manipulate it, make judgements based on it. If you have high 'g' rejoice. If your 'g' is low, tough. You will probably not be smart enough to make it.

But recently this view has been challenged. Books have started to appear with such titles as *The Society of Mind*, *Frames of Mind*, *Multimind*, and *Beyond IQ*. Their central thesis is that there is not just one intelligence, but many. To be no good at conventional intelligence tests does not mean that you are stupid. It may, in fact, point towards other, more useful, intellectual skills. In this chapter we will look at these new theories, and consider whether we have one mind or many.

Measuring the mystery

By intelligence the psychologist understands inborn, all-round intellectual ability. It is inherited or at least innate, not due to teaching or training, it is intellectual, not emotional or moral, and remains uninfluenced by industry or zeal; it is general, not specific, ie, it is not limited to any particular kind of work, but enters into all we do or say or think. Of all our mental qualities, it is the most far-reaching . . . Fortunately it can be measured with accuracy and ease.

The speaker is the distinguished – and at the same time infamous – Cyril Burt, a powerful force in educational psychology in Britain after World War Two, whose ideas on intellectual merit and how it is shaped were influential in the lives of millions of schoolchildren. The date is 1933 and, although over half a century has elapsed, there is much in what Burt said then that remains today's orthodoxy. Many would agree with him that intelligence is something with which one is born (or not, as the case may be) and that, being innate, it is fairly fixed and easy to measure.

Burt was a complex and, in many ways, compassionate individual whose academic methods have recently been shown to be less than honest. But let us not throw out the baby with the bathwater. He reminds us that intelligence is not just something you display during a school or college examination. It enters into everything we say and do. Remember the loquacious Phil in full flight in his street market. Moreover Burt, who was responsible for the testing and selection of bright schoolchildren for grammar-school education in post-war Britain, reckoned that an intelligence test was but a prelude to a deep assessment of a person's abilities. 'To take a young mind as it is,' he wrote in 1921, 'and delicately one by one to sound its notes and stops, to detect the smaller discords and appreciate the subtle harmonies, is more of an art than a science.'

Laudable though that sentiment might be, Burt must still be placed in that long line of behavioural scientists who attributed a profound, some would say unshakeable, importance to the IQ test as a way of classifying people in a hierarchy of mental capacity. What then do the classic IQ tests measure?

IQ tests: the testers tested

IQ testing began in the early years of this century with the French psychologist Alfred Binet and the American Lewis Terman who conceived of an 'average' person's IQ – Intelligence Quotient – of 100. Any variation up or down would therefore be an above or below average score. In formulating such tests they were echoing a suggestion made by the Greek philosopher Plato, who in his celebrated *Republic* had reasoned that, because people differ from each other in their natural mental endowments, they should be subjected to methods of assessment. Only then could one tell which individual would be suitable for one occupation, and which for another. However, it was not so much a Greek philosopher that we might identify as Binet and Terman's true intellectual ancestor as the nineteenth-century academic Francis Galton. Galton was interested in the way in which heredity might shape the differences among humans in much the same way as Darwinian natural selection determined observed variations in the physical characteristics of animal species. In fact Galton himself devised a few simple tests of sensory skill, but it was left to Binet, and later Terman, to measure more complex mental processes culminating in Intelligence Quotient – IQ.

The basic test is a general measure of ability on a variety of tasks. Typically, the subject is tested with vocabulary items to measure understanding, arithmetical problems, visual and spatial tasks, problem-solving involving simple algebra, multiple choice questions, 'creativity' tests to see how far a person can break out of conventional patterns of thought and so on. Since Binet's time there have been many variations on these themes: some for trying to spot high-flying candidates for top jobs in industry; others designed for very young children with limited linguistic or computational skill.

The logic behind these tests is rooted in a simple principle. But, according to Earl Hunt, it contains a fallacy. 'We are presumed,' he writes, 'to know who is intelligent and to accept a test as a measure of intelligence if it identifies such persons.' In other words, intelligence tests measure the ability of people to do well in intelligence tests. When devising tests, researchers tend to validate individual items against the performance of individuals of a certain presumed intelligence. If the item conforms to this presumption it is valid. If not it is discarded. As Hilary Putnam puts it: ' . . . the IQ was "validated" by selecting the items so that they would predict "success" in college – (and thus) is 100% a statistical artefact of this method of validation.'

Obviously there is an element of 'circularity' in this procedure which opponents of intelligence testing are quick to criticize. What they are objecting to, perhaps, is not just that tests do not measure all that we might term 'intelligence' but that they purport to be 'objective' assessments, a clean, cold, clinical instrument that cannot give a biased answer.

But distortion is precisely what the conventional method of validating test items produces, according to two researchers at the School of Education in the British Open University, R. Richardson and J. M. Bynner. They argue their case with a telling analogy. 'Imagine we were to dictate in advance that the whole universe rotated around the earth and we would only accept measures of planetary motion etc. that conformed to this picture. Such dogma was of course the subject of Galileo's struggle against authority. We now look back with pride on the ultimate defeat of such nonsense.'

Despite the harsh judgement of history, Binet's test and variants on it have been very successful. They have also fuelled political and social controversies which are still with us – albeit rather muted. What they led to in psychology, though, was the idea that intelligence could be assessed along a single scale. This idea became one of the cornerstones of modern psychology. Yet it is probably fundamentally misconceived.

IQ testing was taken up with alacrity, particularly in the United States. Lewis Terman at Stanford University developed a version tailored to America, which came to be called the 'Stanford-Binet' test. Upon the results of the test across the country, Terman constructed a social ranking based on IQ. He found that 'borderline' mental deficiency was particularly apparent among Spanish–Indian and Mexican families. He suggested that racial differences in mental abilities would have to be exposed to scientific investigation. It is difficult to avoid the feeling that Terman knew what he wanted to find – that anyone not of 'pure' American stock was a mental defective.

Terman was nothing if not fair, however. Not wishing to exclude the poor, he also found that they were very likely to suffer from impaired intelligence. Terman was supported in his views by other eminent psychologists of the time, notably Henry Goddard and Robert Yerkes. Their pronouncements found a willing audience in America – an audience that welcomed the ability of psychology to tell them the rightful order of the world. In his book *The Science and Politics of IQ*, Leon Kamin points out that: 'The measurement of the fixed mental level was to have a role in determining who was set free and who was jailed; and it was to aid in determining who was sufficiently fit to be allowed to reproduce.'

The influence of the eugenic mental testers was profound. Their results provoked the formulation – and occasional passing – of state laws designed to prevent intellectual undesirables from passing on their faulty 'intelligence genes' to their children. It also influenced American immigration policy. The racial slur that certain countries produced inferior people was enshrined in statute. The Johnson-Lodge Immigration Act of 1924 established quotas for immigrants, based on the idea that people from certain countries had certain intellectual powers. These quotas were based on the census of 1890, which established the racial origins of the American public. From 1924, only 2 per cent of each of these racial groups were to be allowed to settle in the USA. The irony of the use of the 1890 census was not lost on Professor Kamin: 'The "New Immigration" had begun after 1890, and the law was designed to exclude the biologically inferior D– and E peoples of south-eastern Europe . . . The law, for which the science of mental testing must claim substantial credit, resulted in the death of literally hundreds of thousands of victims of the Nazi biological theorists. The victims were denied admission to the United States because the "German quota" was filled.' Science had been subverted to support an arbitrary and inequitable social system. A sorry chapter indeed. Here follows another.

The strange case of Cyril Burt

Sir Cyril Burt's speciality was twins, identical twins, raised separately from one another. In fact he studied 53 pairs of them, a very large number considering their scarcity. (About one pair of identical twins occurs in every 300 births.) Burt claimed that he had evidence that the IQs of identical twins raised apart were also nearly identical. The implication was that the major component of intelligence was hereditary, handed down from the parents. Burt's findings were used to bolster many other claims, particularly Arthur Jensen's that there are inherited and persistent differences between American blacks and whites.

Burt eventually came to grief. His statistics turned out to be too good – the correlation between IQ for pairs did not change as it should have done as the number of pairs studied increased. It also emerged that Burt had falsified certain data on which his findings rested.

The importance of Burt's fakery is that much of what he set out is still accepted as true. He was one of the pioneer devotees of a mathematical technique called 'factor analysis', which was first applied to the study of intelligence by Charles Spearman in 1904. It is an abstruse statistical technique which seeks to extract common factors from a mass of data. In the case of intelligence, these data might include performance on a battery of different tests of intelligence. It comes as little surprise that those who do well on one test also do well on another. Spearman noted this fact, and began to wonder if it did not imply some common underlying ability which was revealed by all tests of intelligence. From his analysis, Spearman proposed that there existed a thing he called 'g', or general intelligence, as well as a set of more specific – and less crucial – attributes. In a paper published in 1904, and titled 'General Intelligence objectively determined and measured', he said: 'All branches of intellectual activity have in common one fundamental function . . . whereas the remaining or specific elements seem in every case to be wholly different from that in all the others . . . This g, far from being confined to some small set of abilities whose intercorrelations have actually been measured and drawn up in some particular table, may enter into all abilities whatsoever.'

Cyril Burt was a devoted disciple of Spearman. Throughout his career he sought to use the concept of 'g' to reinforce his view that intelligence is primarily inherited. His twin studies seemed to prove it. When they were shown to be based on false data, it was not only Burt whose reputation was destroyed: 'g' itself, once seen as the unifying factor common to all intelligence, was discredited. In fact, the disappearance of controversy about the inheritance of intelligence as a major issue almost exactly follows the discrediting of Sir Cyril Burt.

The realization that 'g' was not a particularly useful concept, or might not, in fact, even exist, prompted some psychologists to seek other ways to explain how intelligence might work. Prominent among them are Howard Gardner and Robert Sternberg.

The Trinity of Intelligence – Robert Sternberg

The point to be made . . . is that intelligence is not a single thing: it comprises a very wide array of cognitive and other skills. Our aim in theory, research, and measurement ought to be to define what these skills are and to learn how best to assess and train them, not to figure out a way to combine them into a single, possibly meaningless number.

The triarchic theory of human intelligence seeks to specify the loci of human intelligence and to specify how these loci operate in generating human behaviour . . . The triarchic theory of intelligence is a theory of individuals and their relations to their internal worlds, their external worlds, and their experiences as mediators of the individuals' internal and external worlds.

Robert Sternberg appears to like simple things. In his office at Yale University is a helium balloon painted with a face and with paper legs and arms. It is so cunningly weighted that it sits just touching the floor. Brush it and it will move a couple of feet before stopping to grin at you. 'He's good company,' says Sternberg. On his door is a sign with a moveable arrow. You can choose between 'In', 'Out', 'Engaged', and 'Use your discretion'. The simplicity, however, is deceiving. His triarchic theory is not only a new way of looking at how intelligence might operate, it also seeks to encompass the strengths of preceding theories while excluding their failings. It has another feature. Conventional intelligence tests rely on subjective judgements of what constitutes intelligence. Binet arrived at his IQ test by posing problems to schoolchildren. He took as his baseline the answers of those children the teachers *said* were bright. Unlike other researchers, Sternberg does not deny that what we call intelligence depends to some extent on our judgements of what it is. His theory therefore embodies the commonsense observations of lay people about what intelligence might be.

Implicit theories of intelligence are those that we all have in our heads and use to make our own judgements about the capabilities of ourselves and others. These theories do not have to be constructed, they have to be teased out and made explicit. Sternberg set out to do this by a simple method – he asked people what they thought constituted intelligence. A group that included professors of art, business, philosophy and physics, as well as lay people, was asked to list the characteristics they thought exemplified an ideally intelligent person. The results were interesting. It came as little surprise that the group valued problem-solving ability, verbal skills, logical thinking powers, and a well-stocked mind. In fact, these are all things measured by conventional intelligence tests.

Less expected was the value placed on *practical* aspects of intelligence. Thus, the group thought that intelligent people also had to be able to direct their efforts towards certain goals – they had to be motivated. And they had to be able to demonstrate their intelligence in solving everyday problems, not in the rarefied heights of academic excellence. These attributes are certainly not the province of IQ tests. Sternberg took the view that any theory that attempted to explain intelligence, and any tests that claimed to evaluate it, could be broadened and enriched by taking account of these implicit insights. At the same time, he continued his work on explicit, scientific theory formulation, work which led him to the triarchic theory.

The triarchic theory of intelligence
Sternberg had noticed that most of the existing theories of intelligence could explain reasonably well what was going on in certain restricted areas of thinking. What was needed was some form of more comprehensive, over-arching assembly. As its name implies, the theory has three components. The first provides mechanisms for intelligent behaviour. It has itself three components. The first of these he calls 'metacomponents', or 'executive processes'. These

processes enable us to decide on the true nature of the problems confronting us, and to select the appropriate way of dealing with the problems. The second are 'performance components', or 'non-executive processes'. These are the mechanisms that actually operate when a problem is being solved. The third he terms 'knowledge-acquisition' components. These processes act to acquire new information.

The second part of Sternberg's theory focuses on when intelligence is most apparent. He suggests that intelligent behaviour is most easily seen when individuals are confronted with something new, or when they have managed to reduce their responses to particular aspects of the world to automatic processes – what he calls 'automatization'.

The third part explores the interface between intelligence and the outside world. As Sternberg puts it:

> I think that intelligent behaviour is ultimately behaviour that involves adaptation to, selection of, or shaping of people's real-world environment. Adaptation occurs when a person attempts to achieve a 'good fit' with the environment he or she is in. Selection occurs when a person decides to find a new environment rather than adapt to the one he or she is in . . . Shaping of the environment occurs when a person cannot find (select) an environment that seems suitable.

One of the attractions of the triarchic theory is that it takes account of all three aspects of intelligent behaviour: what goes on inside our heads, our internal world; what happens outside us, the context of intelligence; and what we learn by experience. There has been a heated debate between those who believe that intelligence is wholly inside our heads, and those who say that it makes no sense to consider the phenomenon without reference to the environment in which it operates. Sternberg's view is that this debate is arid:

Diehard contextualists will continue to argue that intelligence inheres only in the environment; diehard mentalists will seek to understand intelligence only with respect to the mental structures and processes of the individual. The debate will never be resolved in this form, because the debate is only in the minds of the theorists and in the contexts they create. Contextual and mentalistic views of intelligence are complementary, not contradictory. Intelligence inheres in the individual and the environments that the individual inhabits.

Sternberg is able to advance a mass of evidence in support of his ideas.

Among the tests Sternberg has applied are those to see whether predictions made by the theory about the way people will deal with new experiences are correct. One test involves asking a group of people to try to assess from photographs of two other people what the nature of their relationship might be. The photographs show two people who really are involved with each other, two who are not, and actors acting as if they were and were not. Triarchic theory predicts some 15 or so measures that people might apply to judge the relationships. The results indicate strongly that the theory has certain predictive powers. Sternberg argues that it can account for the workings of inductive reasoning, deductive reasoning, and acquisition of verbal comprehension, and social and practical intelligence, among other factors. These add up to a comprehensive list of intelligent behaviours. So, for instance, when we are exposed to some new situation we usually have to respond in a novel way – we adjust. Similarly, we are all also capable of reducing valuable skills to automatic processes: reading, say, or driving a car. In Sternberg's theory, these two acts lie at the junction between two elements of the triarchic theory. Dealing with novelty and automatization 'form an important part of what is required in environmental adaptation, selection, and shaping. From the standpoint of the triarchic theory, the regions of environmental experience involving coping with novelty and automatization of processing are those most crucial to intelligence.' He gives other examples of how each of his sub-theories relates to the others, and to the whole.

Sternberg concludes: ' . . . the triarchic theory is an attempt to account for, in a single theory, what in the past has been accounted for by multiple theories often perceived to be in conflict with each other. According to the present view, past theories were often subsets of what a comprehensive theory of intelligence should have comprised. The triarchic theory seems to be at least a step toward such a more comprehensive theory.'

Achievement styles

Everyone envies John. At sixteen and a half he seems to be cruising effortlessly through school, excelling not only in the classroom (where he is invariably at or near the top in most subjects) but also as a sportsman and musician. Being a pleasant sort of individual, his social life too, as you can imagine, is pretty satisfactory. James, his classmate, is also highly intelligent. In fact on a recent IQ test he scored an impressive 131, three points above John. James, like John, does very well in his academic work, getting among the highest grades. And he too enjoys some success in sports and other extra-curricular activities. Now, viewed from the outside, James and John are very similar indeed. But, as all their teachers and friends know, they are really quite different. Where John seems to breeze effortlessly through his many commitments at work and play, James is one of nature's grinders. He succeeds by dint of sheer hard work.

His natural shrewdness tells him what is needed to succeed and his determination ensures that he does so.

James has none of John's flair for grasping quickly the essentials of a problem. He does well by compensating through sheer tenacity. If their teachers were to sum up the stylistic difference in the two boys' abilities they would probably use the word 'insight'.

The role of insight
'We propose', write Janet Davidson and Robert Sternberg, 'that a distinctive characteristic of the intellectually gifted is their exceptional insight ability.' Davidson and Sternberg have carried out a detailed investigation of this quality we call 'insight' and where it fits in the constellation of abilities that characterize the exceptionally gifted individual.

They did so against a background of two basic views of intellectual giftedness. The first is the 'psychometric' or continuum view. This contends that the gifted person is one who possesses greater amounts of – and thus higher scores on measures of – latent mental abilities. These abilities are usually measured on some form of test such as that for general intelligence ('g') or for more specific qualities such as verbal reasoning, visual-spatial ability and so on. Thus the gifted child, from the psychometric viewpoint, is one who does better than an average child on such standard tests.

The second underlying view of giftedness is the 'information-processing' model. Here the idea is not to single out the gifted by what they do in tests so much as to understand the process by which they do it. Presumably the gifted person has superior information-processing skills. He or she can be expected, for example, to retrieve from memory the generic word for warm-blooded animals that suckle their young – mammals – more quickly than the ungifted. Sternberg and Davidson's investigations have been based on this second line of approach: they have been unravelling the processes involved in insightful thinking.

They argue that all significant intellectual accomplishments, such as new scientific theories or major literary and philosophical works, almost always involve major insight. The thinker seems gifted with an ability to get to the heart of a problem in a non-entrenched way rather than by simply processing information rapidly or by displaying the usual IQ test abilities of logic, verbal skill, or visual cleverness. They go on to identify the elements of insight as:

'selective encoding': the ability to sort wheat from chaff, to select what is important from irrelevant information in resolving a problem. When Alexander Fleming's bacterial culture growing in a dish was 'spoiled' by a mould that killed the bacteria, he saw that this was important information. He did not regard the intrusive mould as irrelevant. Indeed he saw that an agent which could kill bacteria could be valuable. When Howard Florey applied some similar thinking to the phenomenon the outcome was the widely used drug penicillin.

'selective combination': the ability to put together isolated pieces of information into an important whole that may not resemble its parts. Darwin's theory of evolution by natural selection was not created from nothing. The component ideas that go to make it up had been around for some time. Darwin's insight lay in synthesizing them.

'selective comparison': the ability to relate newly acquired information to information already acquired in the past. This is the sort of process that a skilled detective goes through when he compares a present case to a former one, or a doctor when he recalls a previous patient with symptoms similar to the one in hand. The famous historical example here is of Kekulé, who discovered the ring-like structure of benzene. In Kekulé's case he was able to link a dream he had had of a snake biting its own tail with the problem in chemistry he had been working on during the day. He saw the snake as a visual image of a molecule.

The many minds of Howard Gardner

Howard Gardner's office at Harvard does not contain any floating men. What it does have is the sounds of children playing next door – an appropriate background for a department of education. Gardner is fond of Martians. They crop up in his writings with some frequency. Their purpose is to point out the limitations of our conventional views of intelligence. Consider, says Gardner, the proverbial Martian visitor to Earth. He – or it – is interested in the intelligence of the human race. Is it likely that he will spend time deliberating over the numbers produced by IQ tests? Gardner thinks not. More probably, the Martian will be drawn to those that perform exceptionally well in particular fields – the chess master, the conductor, perhaps even the athlete. It is undeniable that we consider these accomplished people to be intelligent. Why then do our methods of assessing intelligence often fail to identify them? Gardner's Martian experiment has led him to develop over a number of years an alternative theory of mind and intelligence. He was concerned not to base his ideas on any particular way of testing intellect, or indeed on any cultural preconceptions of what it might be. He is convinced, for instance, that the immensely skilled Polynesian navigator is at least as bright as the straight-As college student, even though their scores on any existing IQ test will be widely different.

Multiple intelligences
As befits an educationalist, Gardner's theory has a purpose. He wants to find a way to bring out the best in each

individual. The theory of Multiple Intelligences allows him to do exactly that. Its central idea is that there is not one intelligence, but many. If we look at the abilities displayed by exceptional members of society, we see that must be so. For instance, is the ability to write a poem the same in principle as the ability to run a large corporation? Clearly not. So within each of us. Many of the things we do that we call intelligent do not exploit the same mental qualities. In fact, there exists a set of abilities, talents and mental skills which, taken together, can be called 'intelligences'.

A definition: in Gardner's view: 'An Intelligence is an ability or set of abilities that permits an individual to solve problems or fashion products that are of consequence in a particular cultural setting.' His research emphasizes the value of the unusual in discovering the underlying foundations of intelligence. So Gardner looked at the normal development of intelligence, and also at prodigies, *idiots savants*, children with learning problems and certain mental disabilities. He explored what different cultures have to say about the concept of intelligence. He did not, though, ignore existing psychological research, particularly into how to teach people a skill, and what the general benefits of skill acquisition might be. Do trained mathematicians make better poets or musicians, for instance?

Putting all his data together he came up with seven Intelligences.

- Linguistic – the sort shown in the extreme by poets.
- Logical–Mathematical – not only displayed in logic and mathematics, but in science generally.
- Spatial Intelligence – the ability to hold in the head a model of the organization of the world around you.
- Musical Intelligence.
- Bodily–Kinaesthetic – the sort shown by, say, dancers.

The use of the whole or parts of the body to fashion some product.
• Interpersonal Intelligence – the awareness of how to get along with others.
• Intrapersonal Intelligence – self-knowledge.

Each of these intelligences is firmly rooted in the mechanics of the brain. Each of them is sensitive to external stimuli that are appropriate to it. Gardner gives the example of sensitivity to harmonies as central to musical intelligence, or to the sounds of words as being vital to linguistic intelligence. Another vital relationship is that between the intelligences and the generation of symbols. The production of a symbol system allows people to work together. It may, in fact, be one of the main characteristics of human intelligence that it works towards making symbols.

Symbol systems are, of course, culturally influenced. The talismans of one culture may be meaningless to another. Multiple Intelligence Theory also takes this into account. Thus Linguistic Intelligence might, in one culture, lead to writing, whereas another might have a tradition of spoken story-telling. Spatial Intelligence might manifest itself as navigational ability in the South Seas, or as hunting in Africa.

Like Sternberg, Gardner is able to marshal an impressive array of evidence to support and develop his ideas. In the case of Musical Intelligence, he points out that the existence of child prodigies supports the notion that musical ability is present from birth in some children. Another line of evidence comes from autistic children. They cannot speak, but some of them can play instruments with great skill and feeling.

The legendary Babe Ruth serves as an example for Bodily –Kinaesthetic Intelligence. He discovered a profound ability to pitch when only 15 years old, and went on to become both an outstanding pitcher and perhaps the best hitter baseball has yet seen. T. S. Eliot founded his own magazine, *Fireside*. As the editor and only contributor, he apparently wrote eight issues in the space of three days. He was 10 years old. Gardner has no difficulty in finding supporting examples for each of his Intelligences. He stresses that his list may not be complete. He has also considered – and rejected – other forms of intelligence which do not meet his strict criteria. Where do his investigations lead him?

Multiple Intelligence Theory is a very practical theory. It begins with the problems which people actually solve in their day-to-day dealing with the world, and works back to the processes, the intelligences, that must be responsible. The most important consequence, though, is that the intelligences are independent. As we have seen earlier, the whole edifice of mental testing is rooted in the conviction that there is one intelligence, and that it can be measured in an hour or so with a fairly simple test. On this basis, the educational future of children can be decided in such a way that they have no opportunities to develop latent talents not revealed by IQ testing. Gardner believes that this will not do. His theory makes it plain that to be good at mathematics does not mean an equal ability in language or music. And, of course, being no good at Interpersonal Intelligence does not mean an equal disability in dance. He also points out that one intelligence is good, but that many working in concert are better.

> To become a successful violinist requires bodily–kinaesthetic dexterity and the interpersonal skills of relating to an audience and, in a different way, choosing a manager: quite possibly it involves Intrapersonal Intelligence as well. Dance requires skills in Bodily–Kinaesthetic, Music, Interpersonal, and Spatial Intelligences in varying degrees . . . Inasmuch as nearly

every cultural role requires several intelligences, it becomes important to consider individuals as a collection of aptitudes rather than as having a singular problem-solving faculty that can be measured directly through pencil-and-paper tests . . . In fact, it may well be that the 'total is greater than the sum of the parts'.

Intelligence and opportunism

In the 1960s a young designer realized that the newly affluent, home-buying, baby-producing couples of Britain, not to mention students and unmarried, aspiring professionals, needed a different kind of furniture shop. They were tired of sombre emporia staffed by bored salespersons and stocked with dull, traditional sofas and chairs. They were the sort of people for whom duvets, brightly patterned chesterfields and roller blinds would strike a chord. So that is what he gave them in the Habitat chain of shops. Twenty years later the designer, now Sir Terence Conran, sits at the head of a multi-million-pound retailing empire. No one would dispute that Conran is highly intelligent. But here is intelligence of an opportunistic kind. He perceived a market gap and carefully filled it, with singleness of purpose. Similarly the Japanese businessman who conceived of a portable cassette recorder that would not record, specifically to allow fast-moving youngsters to play their favourite music on the hoof. The Walkman is now as ubiquitous as the Hoover. Again opportunism.

In the long catalogue of traits that constitute intelligence there is no doubt that having an eye for a good thing, whether it makes you money or is simply an interesting problem on which to work (and perhaps win a scientific Nobel Prize), has an important place. So too does luck. 'Intelligent people', in the sense that they do something significant, profitable, creative or fascinating, owe their intelligence to being in the right place at the right time, or to catching sight of something valuable out of the corner of their eye. This happened to the theatre director Jonathan Miller when he was once stuck for a design for the set of a new opera production. Sitting in the workshop with his designer, and feeling dispirited at their collective inability to come up with a good idea, Miller happened to glance at a model of a set for his previous production. It was by chance round the wrong way, its back facing him, and in a trice he realized that this was it. The back of the old set would be the front of his new one.

Another trait that Miller shares with many other 'intelligent' people is a capacity for hard work. When we see the product of someone's labours we tend to forget the labour and concentrate on the outcome. But it did not materialize by mental magic. Good ideas in science, or imaginative trends in commerce, come about because someone has taken a problem and worked at it diligently, often over a very long time. It would of course be more heroic if they simply conjured bright thoughts out of the blue, on demand, like rabbits pulled from a hat. But rarely is this the case. The advertising man David Ogilvy has built up an international reputation over many years for coming up with what he terms 'Big Ideas'. But he works ferociously to evolve them. 'If you know of any job that doesn't need hard work,' he says with an ironic smile, 'I wish you'd tell me about it and I'll do it in my next incarnation.'

Ogilvy, though clever, is not complacent about his intellectual gifts. Indeed, he has an important strain of humility which many of his ilk share. Intelligence often means being self-critical while, paradoxically, having confidence in what you are doing. One needs pride in order to maintain high personal standards. But a degree of objectivity about the quality of one's effort is also essential. This is especially true in the strict confines of, say, the business world, where budgets and balance sheets dictate the terms. Behaving intelligently for the businessman might mean finding a reasonably good strategy – not necessarily the best imaginable – that comes within the bounds of the financially possible. Anyone can dream up fancy schemes with unlimited resources to hand. It takes real brains to make silk purses from sows' ears. So skill at improvising, at using and reusing available materials and resources, at seeing worth in apparent junk – all these can quite legitimately be called forms of intelligence.

In other words, intelligent behaviour is all about applying personal qualities of drive and resourcefulness, imagination, risk-taking and so on, to whatever problem you are tackling. We are a long way from the somewhat confined notion of intelligence as represented by 'g'.

Theories of multiple intelligences clearly have profound implications for our educational systems, as well as for the ways in which we assess and test intelligence. We will be looking at these later in the book.

In the meantime, an interesting question is raised. If there are all these intelligences living inside our heads, who, or what, controls them?

The Society of Mind

Part of the answer, at least, might lie in the work and the words of the cognitive scientist Professor Marvin Minsky:

How can intelligence emerge from nonintelligence? To answer that, we'll show that you can build a mind from many little parts, each mindless by itself.

I'll call 'Society of Mind' this scheme in which each mind is made of many smaller processes. These we'll call agents. Each mental agent by itself can only do some simple thing that needs no mind or thought at all. Yet when we join these agents in societies – in certain very special ways – this leads to true intelligence.

Marvin Minsky is probably best known for his work in artificial intelligence – the enterprise directed at making a machine that can think. He was one of the founders of the Artificial Intelligence Laboratory at the Massachusetts Institute of Technology. But he is more likely to be found these days in a striking white-and-glass building, designed by I. M. Pei, housing the Media Laboratory. Like everything Minsky has been involved in, the name is more restrictive than the research programme.

Minsky's ideas are, naturally, coloured by his early work. Of necessity, the pioneers of artificial intelligence had to work with simple systems. In those days, computers might number their complexity in a few thousand connections. It was important that each element do some specific and useful job.

We still do not have a machine that can think. Many argue that we never will have, that people and machines are just too different. Others say that every time we make a machine with some vestige of thought, then the critics move the goalposts. If a machine can do it, they say, then it cannot be 'thinking'.

Minsky has no doubts that machines will be able to think, and if perhaps not next year, then some time fairly soon. And his work on the minutiae of computer systems has led him to see analogies with the way the brain works. He points out that one way to understand how something works is to break it down into smaller and smaller pieces. Understanding how the components work, and how they fit together, leads to understanding of how the whole assemblage operates.

The Society of Mind attempts to explain how the human mind works by postulating the existence of individual components of thought, themselves mindless. These are Minsky's 'agents'. He gives the example of a child building towers out of blocks. In control is an agent called 'Builder'. Builder can call on other, subsidiary agents, such as 'begin', 'add', and 'end'. And each of these can call on others. So 'add' can use 'grasp' and 'move' to rearrange blocks; 'find' can call on 'see', and so on. There exists a complicated and extensive hierarchy of agents with specific abilities.

Minsky argues that the domain of each of these agents can be made so restricted that it does not need its own intelligence. The hierarchy consists of unintelligent elements, yet the end result is something that can build towers out of blocks. How can such an agglomeration of stupidity result in intelligence? The answer is that intelligence here is what philosophers call an 'emergent property'. To do justice to Minsky's ideas would require a book the size of his, some 300 pages. Its importance for our use, though, is that it shows how intelligent behaviour might arise from our own brains. Nerve cells, after all, do not have intelligence of their own. Yet group 100 thousand million of them together and they do. Minsky's analysis shows that minds can emerge from non-minds without having to invoke some mysterious, vital force, breathed in from outside. This view also gives us insight into what is, you might say, minding the store. Surely there must be some sort of overall controlling agent, something we might call 'us'? Minsky calls this the 'single-agent fallacy'. It is wrong, he asserts, to suppose that 'a person's thought, will, decisions, and actions originate in some single centre of control, instead of emerging from the activity of complex societies of processes'.

The notion of mind as an emergent property is a very powerful one. In particular, it will allow us in a later chapter to attack one of the oldest and seemingly most intractable problems in science. What is the relationship between the body and the mind?

3

INSIDE THE
ENCHANTED LOOM

It is reported by Mozart's father that the young Wolfgang Amadeus heard Allegri's *Miserere* just once, whereupon he was able to write out the complete score. Many similar breathtaking stories surround the lives of other great composers and performers who were prodigies in childhood. The Hungarian pianist Erwin Nyireghazi, for example, was impressing the world with his playing, improvisation and musical memory by the age of seven. The great mathematician Gauss astonished his schoolteacher by performing what appeared to be a lightning calculation while still a junior. Actually, Gauss was even cleverer than that. He had managed to find a way of reducing what to his classmates was a long addition sum to a simple piece of arithmetic by means of a neat, and original, formula.

It is difficult to read reports of some calculating or musical prodigy without concluding that he or she has a 'superior' brain, a Rolls Royce model in terms of neuronal apparatus, compared to the Ford or Citroën the rest of us possess. And, we reason, even if the super-intelligent do not have better brains in terms of components, they must at least think differently from the rest of us. If the parts are the same, the process must be superior. How true are those assumptions? Let us start with the Mozarts and the Shakespeares, who enjoy the benefits of being 'creative'.

Creativity and IQ
Creative people – in the arts, sciences or wherever – are undeniably intelligent by any criteria. They display a whole range of intelligences in the senses that Howard Gardner uses the term: linguistic, visual and spatial, bodily–kinaesthetic, interpersonal and so on. There is evidence to suggest that what links all the many forms of creativity may be an ability to define and solve problems, which involves high levels of conceptualization, judgement, and self-expression. They

may also score very highly on the relatively restricted criteria of a standard IQ test.

What then is the precise relationship between intelligence and creativity? Michelangelo could be said to be highly intelligent in a creative way or highly creative in an intelligent way. Both 'intelligence' and 'creativity' are terms that help to define each other. Are they then merely aspects of one another which we have cloaked in convenient language? Are they, in short, pretty well synonymous?

B *plus beats a straight* A

According to the British psychologist Liam Hudson, creativity and intelligence are far from being one and the same. Indeed, there is evidence to suggest that, in order to generate original, innovative and valuable concepts, one can have too much of a good thing so far as IQ is concerned. Many, if not most, Nobel prizewinners in science, Hudson points out, have not had outstandingly brilliant school careers. They typically cruise along, picking up competent marks around the B+ level, and often seem to their teachers to underachieve. However, given a problem which interests them, they show unusual powers of concentration and tenacity in resolving it. Once their attention and imagination are fired, they rise to unprecedented heights.

This suggests that the creative individual, given a baseline intelligence that puts him in the Class One stream – say around 120 points on an IQ test – achieves not in direct proportion to 'intelligence', but for strategic or motivational factors. Being obsessed by a physics problem, or passionate about getting a piece of sculpture to express an inner conviction, is simply more important than being top of the class. Liam Hudson offers the analogy of learning to spell. Without being able to write down words and string them together one could not, for example, attempt to write a novel. On the other hand, the mere possession of an ability to spell will not automatically make one a novelist. Similarly, one needs a certain amount of intellectual facility in order to begin to tackle a creative task, but one has to look beyond that basic toolkit for the wherewithal for completing it. 'That the conventional intelligence test', wrote Hudson, 'has failed to predict who will do outstanding work in science (or in any field) there is little question.'

In the drive to be creative, then, in the motivational and personality factors that impel writers and musicians to spend enormous amounts of time and energy on their chosen field, we can see the true factors that separate the 'genius' from the rest of us. There is no mystery of creativity beyond this.

As it happens, psychologists investigating the thinking processes that characterize creative or gifted people tend to spend less time studying normal individuals than they do on those rare but astonishing people who in most respects, except their giftedness, are well below the norm.

Idiots savants

In 1889, Langdon Down (after whom Down's Syndrome was named) brought a new phrase into currency among psychologists interested in mental subnormality. This was 'idiot savant' – 'wise idiot' – and it referred to those remarkable individuals with low general IQ who are unusually gifted in one narrow field of activity. It might be music, art or mathematics. Or it may be an ability to remember vast amounts of information using mnemonics, or to display exceptional spatial skills. Take, for example, Harriet. She had an IQ of 87 at the time she was tested, aged 40, and had spent practically all of her adult life working as a kitchen hand in a hospital. Although Harriet had never had a single music lesson she learned the piano at the age of four and could, it is said, play practically anything from memory after only one hearing. Then there are the 'calendrical calculators' who are able, at astonishing speed, to name the day of the week of any given date. Arithmetically gifted *idiots savants* can in a matter of seconds multiply three-figure numbers, extract square roots or calculate geometric series to 64 places. Such feats make an impressive party trick, but the study of the individuals who perform them may have a wider significance in helping to unravel what goes on in the minds of anyone – low IQ or not – with exceptional intellectual gifts.

According to one estimate in America, 0.06% of the mentally retarded population in residential accommodation may possess special skills in this kind, with calendrical and mathematical ability being most prevalent. That being so, there is a fairly big population on which to draw for experimental purposes, and so far these studies seem to be paying off handsomely in shedding light on the underlying mental processes involved in displaying a special gift. Some of these studies are worth a close look.

Calendrical calculators
At the Medical Research Council's Developmental Psychology Project, housed in the London Institute of Education, Dr Neil O'Connor and his colleagues have for some years been carrying out investigations into the strangely uneven minds of *idiots savants* in various fields. One such series of experiments involved eight subjects, all with intelligence levels well below average, who were able to name the day of the week on which any date falls. Now there are various ways in which this might be done. One relies very heavily on rote learning; the *idiot savant* calculator is able, perhaps, to commit vast tracts of calendrical information, year after year, to a receptive memory. An alternative explanation for Dr O'Connor to consider was that calendrical calculators operate so quickly by having developed a highly practised skill. If the latter is true then this is truly a remarkable skill being demonstrated.

'For example,' writes Dr O'Connor, 'one method of calculating involves starting with the last two digits of the years involved, dividing these by four and adding the integer part to the dividend, ignoring the remainder. A number between 0 and 6, representing the indicated month, is then added and, finally, the day of the month is added to the running total. This total is then divided by 7, the result ignored but the remainder noted. This remainder is then used to enter a table of days of the week to obtain the answer.' Another method involves learning three tables, representing days of the week and months of the year, as well as any required number of years. Then a number of calculations are performed to arrive at an answer. Clearly, whatever method is employed, a calendrical calculator has an awesome talent.

A further strategy that might be employed relies on a knowledge of the rules, regularities and redundancies in the calendar. Every 28 years, for example, there are recurring regularities in the structure of the Gregorian calendar, at least within any century. Another interesting fact is that, in any one year, 1 April and 1 July fall on the same day of the week. Could *idiot savant* calculators be making use of this type of information?

Having located eight subjects (six male and two female) capable of answering calendrical questions concerning a wide range of years, Dr O'Connor tested their skills by giving them dates from five different years: 10 and 20 years before the study was carried out, the year of the study itself, and 3 and 10 years ahead. In all they had 45 dates to calculate. Despite their low intelligence they all showed superior calendrical ability. When the results were analysed in detail the researchers concluded that of the three likely strategies – unusual memory; complex formulae; and knowledge of structural regularities in the calendar – it was the last that probably accounted for their rapid answers. It was, they felt, 'impossible' that the *idiots savants* were using complex arithmetical formulae based on a perpetual calendar. Such labyrinthine computations sit uneasily with their general intellectual disposition. So does a rote memory explanation. Memory of this kind requires high storage capacity of a kind rare even in people with normal IQs. Indeed it seems to be a gift of those with high IQs.

The calculators did show a knowledge of rules and regularities, however. One subject knew that 1 April and 1 July fall on the same day of the week. Another knew that 'the 28 years repeat'. Despite their low IQ scores, these subjects clearly had a feel for the rules which helped them in their calculations. Not all the other subjects showed themselves to be aware of the rules with quite the same degree of insight. Indeed, they were often not inclined to reflect on their underlying thought processes. But the inability to formulate a strategy, says Neil O'Connor, does not mean that one is not being used: ' . . . a native speaker may often be unaware or even ignorant concerning the rules of grammar which govern his language. But he will nevertheless use these rules appropriately.'

Several key points emerge from this and other experiments carried out by the London research team. First, calendrical calculators do use rules and regularities as a strategy for naming days, as well as straightforward arithmetical computations. Second, they are unlikely to be relying on rote memory, a fact which is underscored by the fact that for dates in the future they take slightly longer to get an answer. Thirdly, their specific cognitive skills are quite independent of intelligence as measured on an IQ test. Although the *idiots savants* do differ among themselves in having a range of IQs, their bizarre calculating capacities seem to exist on a mental island cut off from the rest of their intellectual functioning.

Musical idiots savants

An appreciation of music is a fundamental human character-istic. From as early as five months it has been determined, by measuring changes in heart rate, that a baby can tell when a familiar tune is being played. By 18 months babies sing spontaneously, making up endless melodies with con-siderable improvisational skill. Some time after the age of five a memory for music develops, whereby the child begins to represent music patterns internally and matches music which has been heard to those internal representations.

According to Hermelin, O'Connor and Lee in their continuing work on *idiots savants*, the recognition and use of underlying patterns in perceiving, performing and composing music would suggest that a person has at least average levels of cognitive functioning: '. . . the recognition of underlying structural features, and the ability to extract them, are processes of abstraction, and abstraction is gener-ally regarded as a central component of the concept of intelligence.' In other words, in theory at least, musical skills seem to presuppose intelligence of the conventional kind. Yet it is possible to find musically gifted individuals who score very low indeed on IQ tests. What then is the nature of their musical aptitude? Is it wholly independent of 'intelligence' as measured in tests?

These are precisely the questions the researchers addressed when they investigated the abilities of a group of normal children gifted for music and five musical *idiots savants* with a mean verbal IQ of 59 – a very low score indeed. One subject was 19 years old and had attended schools for the mentally handicapped until his late teens. He was autistic, with hardly any spontaneous speech, and displayed some 'bizarre and obsessive behaviour patterns'. Outside the pro-tected environment of institutional care he could not sur-vive. Yet from the age of eight he had shown considerable musical ability, playing on the piano anything he had heard on the radio after about three hearings. He had accumulated a large classical repertoire. Another subject was 58 years old, his ability only coming to light when he was over 50. Again he had led an institutional life (he was totally blind from birth); again he showed an exceptional musical talent, this time for composing songs. A third subject was brain-damaged at birth. Now 36, he too grew up in institutions where he showed no desire to communicate. Yet he too could pick up tunes easily, had an extensive knowledge of composers such as Richard Strauss and Schoenberg; could improvise readily and so on. The two other *idiot savant* subjects had similar case histories, uncommunicative or obsessive behaviour coupled with enviable gifts in learning to play, improvising or composition.

Set against those five was a control group of six normal children, average age 13 years, who had received special music tuition but no formal training in composition and improvisation. All the experimental subjects were given five tasks to test their musical inventiveness: continuing a tune; inventing a phrase or tune; improvising an accompaniment to a melody played to them; composing a piece with melody and harmony; improvising in a jazz idiom over a 12-bar blues. The performance of all those taking part was recorded and rated by 'blind' assessors. When the results were ana-lysed, *'idiots savants* who were musically gifted were noted to be far superior to normal controls in both their musical inventiveness and their competence level.'And these gifts seem to be independent of their performance on standard IQ tests.

Intelligence and mental speed

IQ tests are, as we have seen, fraught with dangers. They have been above all accused of being arbitrary, because they seem to reflect not so much real differences between people as narrow types of ability determined by accidents of birth. In the words of a publication from the British National Union of Teachers: 'The definition of "intelligence" seems to rely on criteria which are subjective and social rather than objective and scientific.' If these differences persist throughout childhood into adult life it is because, the opponents of IQ tests argue, variations in social and educational opportunities also persist: and IQ scores reflect these injustices.

For many years now psychologists have been looking for another measure of intelligence which would be beyond the criticism of IQ tests by being wholly objective. For this they have turned to the information processing capacities of the brain. Smart people, the reasoning goes, probably figure out things faster than those who are less intelligent. Their brain cells probably respond more quickly when confronted with a task. Could it not be then that a fairly simple criterion such as reaction time correlates broadly with intelligent behaviour?

For over half a century experimenters have been trying to test the truth of that proposition. Typically, they sit a subject in front of a small row of buttons. Behind each of these is a light that comes on at random. When any light comes on the subject has to release a 'home button' and press the appropriate button in front of a light. The time it takes to release the home button is termed 'movement time'; and to press the target light button the 'response time'. Together they make up the subject's reaction time or RT. When this has been determined for a number of subjects a chart is drawn up logging RT against IQ. For a time in the early days it seemed as if such correlations were solid, but subsequently doubts have crept into the minds of other researchers. It could be, for example, that what gives a person a fast reaction time is not that he or she has a basic underlying superiority in mental processing speeds, but an

ability or willingness to concentrate for a fair time on what
is an essentially boring task of pushing buttons. Moreover,
in experimental variation on the basic theme it is found that
there is greater correlation between IQ and RT if the task is
made more difficult, presumably because more psychological processes are being sampled.

Reaction time experiments, then, have not been
altogether satisfactory. J. P. Das wrote in 1979 that 'many
a researcher has wasted his life in pursuit of a "speed"
measure of intelligence', while a year later E. Hunt offered
the opinion that 'the search for a "true" single information-
processing function underlying intelligence is likely to be as
successful as the search for the Holy Grail.'

Inspection Time
Nevertheless, researchers have persisted with the idea that
such a function could underlie intelligence and they have
come up with a variant on RT called Inspection Time – IT.
The equipment used is the tachistoscope which enables the
experimenter to present a subject with a very brief visual
stimulus and to elicit a response. At Edinburgh University,
for example, Dr Ian Deary carried out a series of tests in
which subjects were shown two vertical lines, one longer
than the other. The longer line would rapidly appear either
on the left or the right and subjects had to state which as
soon as the lines appeared. To perform such a task requires
very little active thought. The IT is purely a measure of a
person's speed of intake of information – in this case about
the relative positions of black pencil lines drawn on white
card. When Dr Deary's subjects had recorded their ITs he
then set these alongside their IQ scores and found an
impressive correlation. And he is not the only researcher to
do so. In the relatively short time that IT has been investigated at least nine studies have pointed in the same direction.
What is more, the link between IT and IQ seems to hold

true for a diversity of groups with a wide spread of intelligence: young children; mentally handicapped people; college students; a random adult population.

A similar finding emerges from inspection time tests where the stimulus is not visual but auditory. Two tones of markedly different pitch are played, and the subject has to state low–high or high–low according to the protocol of the experiment. Again responses correlate well with the subjects' IQ scores.

All this is not to say that IT is a totally reliable measure. It is far from being the Holy Grail. For one thing, there is the question of whether a person with a high IQ does better on the test because he or she is more willing to sustain attention to a boring task. There are also a few technical objections to the way IT experiments have been carried out.

However, taking these caveats into account, and facing the fact that the early hopes of IT have had to be somewhat modified, Ian Deary believes that the simple measure of IT has a great deal to offer: ' . . . the combination of the reliability and size of the IT – IQ relationship, the number of independent groups who have replicated it and the apparent simplicity of the task put IT in a unique position for the study of basic processes in intelligence.'

Quick thinkers in action

Mental speed in processing information does seem, in some circumstances, to differentiate people of normal intelligence – as measured in a variety of ways – from those deemed intellectually gifted. Over a number of years two British psychologists, Hermelin and O'Connor, studied the way in which children of high academic or musical ability cope with various tasks involving rapid decision-making compared to groups of normal control subjects.

In one test of conceptual categorizing the children were

shown pairs of words or pairs of pictures and asked to decide as quickly as they could whether the items belonged to the same or different categories. In another experiment the children had to compare words or pictures which described either synonyms or unrelated items and decide as quickly as possible whether any two items did or did not share a common meaning.

Interestingly, in both sets of experiments, the high IQ groups appear to make faster decisions than the controls, but only when working with words. When pictures are involved there seems to be no difference in decision-making speed between the two groups. Hermelin and O'Connor speculate that this may be because 'the process of picture classification bypasses any lexical or logogen system, whereas when names for pictures have to be found, lexical search and retrieval will become necessary.' If this is so, the argument runs, then the faster one can process the brain's search and retrieval mechanism the more heavily should one score on verbal tasks.

As it happens, an intriguing by-product emerged from these experiments. Hermelin and O'Connor also found that musically gifted children whose IQ scores were no higher than the control groups also outperformed the latter in decision-making when word pairs were involved. Those with unusual musical talents seem to share with highly intelligent children a quality that could be – paradoxically – independent of IQ scores. Perhaps, the experimenters suggest, 'performance level on certain cognitive operations may not depend on level of intelligence, but on the kind of strategy adopted. Different types of strategies may in turn be related to, or determined by, some outstanding specific talent. In this latter instance, different IQ levels within groups of musically or artistically gifted children would be irrelevant to the level of task performance.'

Inside the rapid brain

If intelligence is, in some way, linked to sheer speed of information processing, what factors are involved in determining that speed? To explore this, we need to take a brief look at the way the normal brain processes the vast amount of data it handles all the time: a message transmission and reception system of awesome efficiency.

The human brain is estimated to contain around 100 thousand million cells – neurones – each of which interconnects with thousands of others. The meeting points for nerve cells are vanishingly tiny gaps called synapses, across which pulses of electrical activity are sent when messages are passed through the system. The form these messages take is chemical. An electrical impulse travels from one end of a neurone to the other, where it triggers the release at the synaptic terminal of one of a number of 'neurotransmitters' such as dopamine. Once released, this chemical flows across the gap of the synapse on to the next cells where it activates another electrical impulse. This, in turn, flows through the receiving cell to the synaptic junction with its neighbour, where the whole cycle is repeated.

A number of factors are crucial in maintaining the brain's ability to operate effectively: the conductivity of the nerve fibres that take up the electric impulses; the rate of synthesis of neurotransmitter substances – and the rate at which they are subsequently broken down by specially produced enzymes; the number and type of nerve cells that are brought into play for specific tasks. Thus, for the sort of ultra-rapid processing that might go on in the brains of the highly intelligent, it might be postulated that the manufacture and breakdown of transmitting chemicals takes place with unusual facility. Not only would such people generate necessary quantities of neurotransmitters more quickly than most. They would also rid the system of those substances that have outlived their usefulness – as message carriers – with superior speed, measured in microseconds.

At the University of Toronto, Dr Edward Reed has been studying the action of two proteins in the brain that might indeed affect the speed with which a message-carrying neurotransmitter is synthesized and broken down. The particular neurotransmitter involved is noradrenalin, a chemical which neuroscientists have been investigating for many years as it seems to play an important role in all kinds of inter-neuronal communication. Reed's suggestion – made in the pages of the journal *Nature* – is that there might be variations between individuals in the control mechanisms, as regulated by the genes, that determine levels of the two critical enzymes. Thus the more intelligent person might simply be the one whose genes allow the more rapid production and destruction of noradrenalin by means of the regulatory enzymes.

On the other hand, there is evidence to suggest that this basic 'genetic' control mechanism may not be quite so inflexible as one might think. In the Physiology Department at Oxford University, Dr Marianne Fillenz has shown that, although the enzyme levels controlling the flow of noradrenalin may be under genetic control, they can be modified and manipulated by experience. Using laboratory rats for her experiments, she has been able to demonstrate, for example, that levels of enzyme are increased when the animals are put in mildly stressful situations. A tiny environmental change then increases the brain's ability to process information.

Quick on the uptake

Whatever the precise relationship between genes and environment – nature and nurture – in determining speed of processing, it does seem tempting to infer that the brighter one is, the more efficient is one's neuronal apparatus. The thinking machine seems better lubricated. The recent findings of Dr Richard Haier at the University of California also point in that direction.

Using medical high technology, Dr Haier has been able to overcome a major hurdle in investigating the neurobiology of intelligence: he has been able to study what is going on in the brain of his subjects while they are engaged in intelligent activity. What is more, his subjects are not laboratory rats but humans.

For his non-invasive research, Haier has drawn on the PET scanner – developed originally as a clinical tool to allow doctors to monitor the functioning of the brain in patients with identified or suspected disability. Positron Emission Tomography enables the observer literally to watch the brain in action. Richard Haier injected into three groups of subjects a harmless glucose known as FDG which contained a special radioactive marker. The FDG was taken up by the brain in about 30 minutes, the areas that used the most being those that were metabolically the most active. During the uptake period the different groups were given a number of tasks, including, in the case of eight individuals, an abstract reasoning test. Then the subjects were put under the PET scanner, where it was possible to see how their brains had responded to the radioactive glucose. After a number of analyses and comparisons, Dr Haier was able to show that there was a definite link between glucose metabolic rates and performance on the abstract reasoning task. It was, to use the jargon, an 'inverse correlation'. In other words, the higher the score on the test – which forms part of a normal IQ battery – the less glucose the person's brain had used. Intelligence seems here again to mean increased neuronal efficiency. Conversely, those for whom the mental task was clearly difficult needed more neuronal activity – as indicated by higher glucose use – in order to perform it. They were, relatively, inefficient.

With commendable caution, Dr Haier does not claim that these findings and interpretations are conclusive. Quite apart from the tiny population of people investigated, there are a number of unanswered questions. Did those who performed poorly on the IQ task, for example, concentrate badly in the experimental situation? Were they very anxious? Until more such tests are carried out, Richard Haier makes no grandiose claims. But he does suggest that 'intelligence is not a function of more brain activity, but rather efficiency of brain processes relevant to the particular task.'

Brainwaves and IQ tests

In what has become a classic description of the mechanics of the brain, Sir Charles Sherrington took as his starting point an analogy drawn from the weaving industry. The brain is like 'an enchanted loom, where millions of flashing shuttles weave a dissolving pattern, always a meaningful pattern though never an abiding one, a shifting harmony of sub patterns. It is as if the Milky Way entered upon some cosmic dance.' Now every generation draws its own analogues. The 'flashing shuttles' comparison inevitably gave way to the telephone exchange metaphor, in which the brain was seen as a central message sender/receiver. Today we prefer to think in terms of the silicon chip, with small pulses of current switching devices on and off to forge the numbers of binary arithmetic, like neurotransmitters exciting or inhibiting nerve cells. Whatever the metaphor, Sherrington's evocative lines bring home to us the highly dynamic nature of the brain. It is all action, ceaseless even in sleep (when, indeed, it may at times be hyperactive) and charged with patterns.

For some 60 years now a useful tool for observing these

changes and determining those patterns has been the electro-
encephalogram – the EEG machine. Since the 1930s researchers have been trying to discover, for example, whether
the brain's electrical activity – as recorded on the EEG –
might in any way relate to a person's intelligence as established by a psychometric test. Is there a connection between
patterns of brain waves and known IQ? Many experiments
have been conducted with this question in mind, but the
results, until fairly recently, have tended to be inconclusive,
even contradictory. Typically these experiments measure a
subject's electrical reaction to a stimulus. These Evoked
Potentials (EP) are represented as a waveform on the EEG.
Detailed examination of the characteristics of the waveform
shows differences between individuals. In some tests these
differences also seem to be a reflection of differences in IQ;
in others there is no such distinction to be made.

A team of researchers at Brown University and Butler
Hospital, Rhode Island, recently carried out its own experiments on a group of 23 nursing students, average age 22.1
years and all but one female. The students were put in a
darkened room in front of a translucent screen. Then lights
lasting half a second each were flashed on the screen at
carefully judged intervals. The lights varied in intensity. All
the subjects were wired to an EEG machine. As the lights
flashed, a recording of their EPs was taken and the waveforms
carefully analysed. A fortnight after this lab work, all the
nursing students were given a well-known test for measuring
intelligence – the Raven's Advanced Progressive Matrices.

When the EP measures and intelligence tests were compared certain intriguing correlations were found. Most importantly, the researchers discovered that the strongest link
was when the intensity of the light stimulus was 'intermedi-
ate'. In other words, when moderate or average stimulus
was given, there was the best fit between IQ score and
the characteristics of EP waveforms. 'This observation',

conclude the researchers, 'supports the view that higher intelligence is a consequence of greater activation of central processes . . . in response to normal levels of stimulation.' In other words, what might differentiate a person of high intelligence from a less intelligent one is the way he or she responds to input from the environment. The more intelligent person simply behaves differently in the way his or her brain's electrical activity reacts to stimulus. 'Perhaps the most startling conclusion . . . is not just that there is a relationship between brain potentials and intelligence, but that the relationship is quite strong.'

The researchers go on to suggest that this lends weight to the proposition that 'the variance of intelligence, with all its complex manifestations, may result primarily from relatively simple differences in fundamental properties of central brain processes.' It is almost like saying that the difference between, say, two companies, one successful, innovative and super-efficient, the other old-fashioned, ailing and losing money fast, is not the result of poor management, weak organization and anachronistic practices so much as the fact that one has air-conditioning and the other does not. An uncomplicated matter of worker comfort, not Harvard Business School expertise, spells success or failure.

Developing intelligence: the brain responds to learning

In 1981 a neuropathologist in Toronto made a discovery with important repercussions among brain researchers in general. Dr Laurence Becker found that the nerve cells in the brains of new-born babies with Down's syndrome developed differently from those of normal neonates. The Down's children's neurones made far fewer synaptic contacts, and hence connections with other nerve cells, and did not mature to the same size. Now Down's sufferers are severely mentally retarded, scoring very low indeed on any measures of intelligence. So Becker had found what might be a cause of their intellectual deficits: they have a reduced capacity to transfer information between nerve cells.

A series of experiments with young laboratory rats yielded similar results. Rats were given a series of tasks to master over the course of a few weeks. Initially these were quite simple, reflex behaviours but, after 25–30 days, they became more complex, such as walking along a narrow bridge. Tissue samples from the animals' brains showed that their synaptic development mirrored closely their behavioural skills. The number of contacts made by cells peaked in phase with the complex tasks and the disc-shaped contact points grew larger as well. Now it could have been simply coincidence: the rats' brain cells were maturing physically just as they were being given tasks to learn. 'But', says Professor Ted Petit, 'a more intriguing possibility was that those cellular changes were responses to acts of learning. The most dramatic neuronal changes had, after all, taken place at a time when the young animals were committing a great deal of new information to memory.'

This very idea had been around since 1949, when the psychologist Donald Hebb had speculated that, when particular brain cells are used in learning, they probably change in structure. Indeed, those changes are probably the way in which memories are stored. At the University of Illinois, Dr William Greenough showed that the more demands one places on newborn animals, so that they are forced to learn to cope with and adapt to their environment, the more connecting nerve fibres and junctions they develop. If deprived of normal stimulus, the brain will, on the other hand, produce fewer synapses than normal.

Again, though, there is the problem of whether increased or decreased learning and stimulation is affecting the normal developmental process of the brain. All Greenough's experiments were again with young, maturing animals. What

Petit and his colleagues have been trying to establish is whether learning exerts an effect on the number and configuration of neurones in the adult brain. From a series of experiments with laboratory rats, Petit tends to infer that it does. When animals are given an injection of a chemical to stimulate synaptic action in roughly the same way that learning would, there is a sudden increase in synaptic diameter and curvature. Other experiments have shown an increase in the number of dendritic spines: ' . . . these physiological changes seem to contribute (as Hebb had speculated they would) to the ability of neurones to relay and receive information. An increase in the number of synapses on a neurone is by definition an increase in the number of avenues by which it can interact with others.'

Quite apart from the inherent interest in unravelling the string of neurophysical events associated with the act of learning (and there is still some way to go yet before the full picture of what happens in the human brain is completed), there are some profound practical implications of this research. The brain of the human baby, both in the womb and during its first couple of years or so of independent life, develops, like children's bodies, in a series of 'growth spurts'. The key spurt begins about 10 weeks before birth, continuing for the next 18–24 months. During this time neurones have a frenzy of increased connectivity with thousands of other nerve cells, sending out fibres in all directions like some prolific tropical plant taking over a greenhouse. The brain grows accordingly in size. At birth it is a quarter of its adult weight; at 6 months one-half; at 2½ years it is three-quarters developed. By the age of 5 the infant's intellectual development is virtually complete. So too is all the basic learning that we will ever do.

If the work of Petit and others is correct in its general conclusions – namely that the power of the brain is governed by the ability of neurones to change their physiology in response to outside stimulation – then these growth phases must be regarded as in a sense the critical juncture at which intelligence develops. That is not to say that by the age of five we are irredeemably locked into an established mental prison from which we cannot hope to escape. That would be unduly pessimistic (or optimistic, according to how lucky an individual might be).

What this period of plasticity in which the brain is establishing the very basis for cognition reminds us is that, to some degree, our intellectual future is very much in our own hands. Studies of malnourished mothers in the Third World reveal that their babies can possess at birth fewer than half the complement of neurones found in Western children. And, in the nutritionally privileged industrialized world, there appear to be 'seasons' for mental retardation. Statistics show a higher incidence of backwardness among babies born in winter months – possibly, though this is highly speculative, because their mothers were more likely to be eating salads than high-protein meals during the previous summer, the start of the brain growth spurt.

Another implication of the findings on growth spurts and neuronal plasticity concerns the stimulation we give young children. The brain seems to thrive on activity: the more it is given to do in these development stages the more powerful it seems to become. There do seem to be differences in the degree of plasticity of one individual compared to another. If this could be measured, indeed, it might even be used as a measure of intelligence itself. However, all youngsters possess the ability to grow, change and respond to stimulus at an early age. Thus it behoves us to explore to the full the kinds of mental experience we might offer them. As we shall see later, the results of deliberately branching into the brain's natural development can be quite extraordinary.

Where is intelligence?

'There's no art,' wrote Shakespeare, 'To find the mind's construction in the face.' Even so, that is precisely what most of us often try to do. We look at another person's face and read in it, or rather project on to it, a notion of what that person is really like or what may be going on inside his or her head. The practice has a long history. For centuries inferences about personality, attitude or intention have been drawn on the strength of the tilt of the nose or the slant of the eyebrow. As for intelligence? Why, everyone knows that a prerequisite is a high forehead in the manner of Bertrand Russell or Albert Einstein. The lofty brow is synonymous with the lofty thinker.

This particular notion stems from the theories of two German anatomists, Gall and Spurzheim, who believed that different regions of the brain carried out specific functions. As we shall see shortly, neuroscientists today believe much the same thing, though with certain important divergences from Gall and Spurzheim. For them the 'intellect' was in a part of the brain right at the front over the eyebrows. Thus, if a person had a big forehead one could assume that his or her forehead was bulging with clever grey matter. For the skull analysts, or cranioscopists, quality was also equated with quantity. Big was beautiful, as far as intellect was concerned.

Now these ideas, together with those of the phrenologists who contended that the various lumps and bumps on the surface of the head were indicators of personality and intelligence, were for some time extremely persuasive. There are people who still subscribe to them today. However, from the scientific point of view, they are about as valid as astrology or spiritual healing. Probably less so, because research has provided a compelling weight of evidence to the contrary.

Firstly, the localization of intelligence in the forehead fell from favour in the 1930s with the work of the Portuguese psychiatrist Antonio Moniz. It was he who pioneered the surgical technique called frontal lobotomy, whereby the frontal part of the brain is removed in an attempt to rid patients of severe psychiatric symptoms. For initiating the technique Moniz was awarded the Nobel Prize. But because many lobotomized patients showed no decrease in intelligence – as measured, say, by an IQ test – Moniz concurrently tolled the death knell for the high forehead lobby.

The second important development concerns brain size. The human brain has an average weight of about 1400 grams. Some brains demonstrably outperform others. The neural apparatus of a Gauss, a Feynman or a Stravinsky operates with more telling proficiency or effectiveness than the brain of most people plucked at random off the street. If two people score 92 and 132 respectively on an IQ test – provided they have been properly selected for cultural bias and so on – there do seem to be biological differences in how their minds work. However, the distinction is certainly not one of sheer size. 'Few neurologists', writes Professor Ted Petit of the University of Toronto, 'could distinguish at a glance between the brain of a genius and that of an idiot. The reason, recent findings suggest, is that intelligence – for our purposes, the ability to learn and remember and to solve problems – is determined not by the overall shape of the brain but by the structure and function of individual neurones, or brain cells.'

If it is possible, then, to pin down intelligence, biologically speaking, we have to focus not on quantity but quality, not on size but on neuronal efficiency. And we need to look for this in the right places. The various regions to which the cranioscopists and phrenologists assigned specific functions are now known to carry out rather different operations.

Compartments of the mind

'I was in an office somewhere. I could see the desk. I was there and someone was calling to me – a man leaning on a desk with a pencil in his hand.'

That apparently innocuous description of past events is in fact one of a number of startling revelations to emerge from the pioneering work of Dr Wilder Penfield and his colleagues at the Montreal Neurological Institute some decades ago. Penfield carried out many hundreds of surgical operations on the brain between 1936 and 1960, during which he tried to ascertain what functions the different areas of the cortex might carry out. His technique was to introduce fine electrodes into different areas of the brain along which a small electric current could run. When particular areas known as the temporal cortex were stimulated in this way, and the patients subsequently asked to report on what they had experienced (no pain was involved, by the way), they frequently called up memories such as that quoted above. Now the specific areas stimulated are probably not precisely the points at which these experiences were originally recorded. The total memory is more widely distributed throughout the brain. However, Penfield's remarkable findings gave a lead to other neuroscientists in mapping the functional regions of the brain. Electrical stimulation is one technique. There are now a few more.

These explorations have given us a pretty reliable guide to the overall architecture of the hundred thousand million or so neurones in the human brain, and shown us how this might have come about in the course of our evolutionary history. In the beginning the brain was simply a number of cells sensitive to information about the basic condition of the environment. A primitive, single-celled organism living in some primeval soup would evolve a mechanism for monitoring the temperature, acidity, pressure and so on of its aqueous medium. With the passing of millions of years these receptor cells would be complemented by further message-carrying cells that also sent back information from the interior to the surface of the creature. There would be a two-way shuttling of information to produce responses and actions in appropriate circumstances and to regulate the organism's behaviour.

In the earliest stages of evolution single-celled, amoeba-like creatures were joined by jellyfish-type animals, then molluscs and ultimately the primitive fish in which the first true 'brains' can be identified, with clusters – or ganglia – of nerve cells and a spinal cord from which nerves radiate all over the body. 'In many respects,' reflects Peter Russell, 'the lower parts of our brain and spinal cord have not changed significantly since the time of the early fishes, 100 million years ago.' But he goes on to add that there was one crucial series of evolutionary changes that characterizes the development of higher animals: the massive extension and enlargement of the top end of the primitive brain – the cerebral cortex – which, in the first mammals to evolve 200 million years ago, grew to occupy half the brain's total volume. It is on the cortex and the overlaying layers of cells called the neocortex that we need to focus, because in the familiar, convoluted folds of the whole cortical region are contained those functions and capacities that separate us from our distant evolutionary ancestors. Here is the seat of our intelligence.

4

MINDS, BRAINS
AND SOULS

What is Matter? – Never mind.
What is Mind? – No matter.
(Punch, 1855)

How . . . could this grey and white gook inside my skull
be conscious?
(John Searle, 1984 BBC Reith Lectures)

How indeed?

The 'mind–body' problem has puzzled, intrigued, and
frustrated philosophers and scientists for centuries. We
know, and have known for some time, that the universe is
composed of particles which interact according to rigid
physical laws. These particles are unthinking and unconscious. Yet we also know that we are conscious, and that
we have a rich internal mental life of thoughts and feelings.
It is not immediately apparent how these two phenomena
can be connected. How can conscious thought arise out of
unconscious, inanimate matter?

There are those who believe that the solution to the
problem is to say that there is no problem. John Searle, for
instance, finds it hard to understand why we think that the
connection between mind and brain presents difficulties,
while nobody worries about, say, a 'stomach–digestion'
problem. We will be coming back to Searle later.

René Descartes was educated as a Jesuit. He had a fairly
unfettered mind, writing on mathematics and philosophy.
He was also, perhaps peculiarly, a soldier. The story goes
that once, on a campaign in Belgium, he found shelter in
a stove. (This was, of course, not what we think of as a stove,
but a large brick-built structure.) Lulled by the warmth, he
fell to thinking. His thoughts led him somehow to his
famous saying: 'I think, therefore I exist.' He had realized
that the fact of his thoughts made it indisputable that he
existed.

Taking this starting point, he went round the collection of the rest of his beliefs. Applying the same logic to each of them he was able to work out which were true, and which were not. Eventually, Descartes found himself in something of a bind. All his theoretical and philosophical musings had enabled him to set out theories in which everything was explained in terms of matter. That is, he held a fairly physical view of the universe. Unfortunately, his education, upbringing, and the social climate at the time also forced him to acknowledge the existence of a beneficent God, overlooking all our activities. The solution for Descartes was to suggest that there are two separate and completely different sorts of phenomena: mental things and physical things. And never the twain shall meet – or at least only under certain special circumstances. Our minds, thoughts, feelings, and so on are in the first category. Our bodies, brains, in fact the rest of the material universe, are in the second.

Cartesian Dualism, as Descartes' theory came to be called, has endured remarkably well. First published in the 1630s, it still attracts distinguished supporters today, despite what has been learned about the physiological basis for most of the things that we consider to be thought.

Descartes' notion neatly sidesteps one of our problems – how do minds arise out of brains – by assuming that they do not. The mind, according to him, does not need the body. But this view in itself causes further problems. Mental causation is one of these. As John Searle puts it: 'We all suppose, as part of common sense, that our thoughts and feelings make a real difference to the way we behave, that they actually have some *causal* effect on the physical world. I decide, for example, to raise my arm and – lo and behold – my arm goes up. But if our thoughts and feelings are truly mental, how can they affect anything physical? . . . Are we supposed to think that our thoughts and feelings can somehow produce chemical effects on our brains and the rest of our nervous systems?'

Descartes himself was aware of this limitation. He proposed to meet it by suggesting that mind and body could 'intermingle', react with each other in some way. How they were to do so was left unsaid.

Cartesian Dualism was very influential. Other thinkers, however, were looking for other ways to solve the problems inherent in Descartes' ideas. Around the turn of the century, William James, for example, set forth the theory of neutral monism, in which the physical world is constructed out of our own sensory experiences. George Berkeley, in the early 1700s, avoided the point altogether by asserting that matter does not exist, a point of view which did not meet with much enthusiasm.

Most recently, discoveries in understanding the processes that go on in our brains when we think are suggesting a more hard-nosed, materialistic theory of the mind. On this view, the operation of the brain and what we conceive of as thoughts are inextricably linked. Thinking becomes merely a manifestation of some activity, chemical or electrical, within the brain. Not surprisingly, most neurophysiologists accept this view, although at least one of the most distinguished does not. The Nobel laureate Sir John Eccles refuses to believe that brains are all there is to minds. He prefers to invoke a spiritual force, a God, that infuses our mental abilities. He is supported in this position by Sir Karl Popper, the equally distinguished philosopher.

Other philosophers disagree. John Searle, Professor of Philosophy at the University of California, Berkeley, is convinced that brains cause minds. In his 1984 Reith Lectures for the BBC and the subsequent book *Minds, Brains and Science*, he argued that the way to dispose of the mind –body problem is to accept that minds are what we have called earlier 'emergent properties' of brains.

Minds out of brains

John Searle seeks to explain a number of puzzles about our human mental experiences. Among them, he sees consciousness as central to being human because: 'Without it all of the other specifically human aspects of our existence – language, humour, love and so on – would be impossible.' He also wants to attack the problem of mental causation which bedevilled Descartes.

Searle draws on much modern biological research to support his argument. Consider, he says, pain. We know that the sensation of any pain we perceive begins as something happening to a nerve somewhere in the body. The signal passes through several stages until it ends up in the brain, in a region called the thalamus, among others. This much we know by tracing the paths of nerves. In fact, it is not even necessary for something to happen to a nerve outside the brain. The pains felt by amputees – phantom limb pains – or those felt when the brain is stimulated directly show this.

We are happy to accept this sort of explanation for pain, which is after all a very mental experience, witness anaesthesia. So why cannot our thoughts appear in the same way? Again, Searle draws on the findings of physical science. Consider the idea of solidity. We have commonsense ideas of what solidity means. It means you can rest your word processor on the table, or eat a meal on it. But the solidity we observe on the large scale is caused by interactions between the atoms that make up the table on the very smallest scale. We therefore have two definitions of solidity: ' . . . solidity just is the lattice structure of the system of molecules and . . . causes, for example, resistance to touch and pressure. Or one can say that solidity consists of such high-level features as rigidity and resistance to touch and pressure and that it is caused by the behaviour of elements at the micro-level.' In exactly the same way, the large-scale observable features of brains – what we call thoughts, or even minds – are caused by activity in the small-scale structure of the brain, in the neurones and their connections.

This theory takes away much of the mystery from minds, and from their relationship to brains. In the same way that stomachs make digestion possible, so brains make minds. They are both biological processes, similar in type. The problems identified earlier then also cease to exist. Consciousness is one of the properties of minds produced by brains. Similarly, mental causation now goes neatly away. Thoughts are no longer ethereal and nebulous. They are rooted in the physical reality of nerve cell firings and synapse action. Their generation and manipulation can be observed by, for instance, brain scanners. It should not be a surprise, therefore, that a thought such as 'arm go up', can result in the arm's actually going up.

Searle's ideas are persuasive because they are anchored in what brain scientists are now telling us about how brains work. We know that neurones function when we think. We know that great areas of the brain act together to perform particular functions. His analogy with the physical sciences is also telling. We do not doubt that a table is solid just because we cannot see the underlying physical activity that causes that property to emerge. Searle also seems to have solved the problem of what consciousness is and where it comes from. It also is just something that brains do. Others, however, are not so sure.

Consciousness and other minds

How do we know that other people have minds in the same way as we do? This is another classic problem in philosophy, and also concerns the nature of consciousness. Part of the problem is our inability to get inside the skulls of other people, to experience directly what goes on in there. We usually have no doubt that we ourselves are conscious, and most of the time we extend the same courtesy to others. It makes it easier to get on with people if we assume that they are experiencing roughly the same thoughts, feelings and emotions as we are. Unfortunately, we have no real, objective, scientific evidence for our belief.

This should not worry us too much. Solipsism – the idea that the only person you really know to exist is yourself – turns out to be interesting but useless. There are also commonsense objections to it. Everything we can see about our fellow human beings leads us to believe that they are just like us. They have thoughts, feelings, desires, pains and so on in their heads in exactly the same way as we do. They are also conscious of them. In fact, it is just about impossible to make sense of the behaviour of other people without making that assumption. Unless, of course, you are prepared to believe that the world is really inhabited by millions upon millions of very clever robots . . .

If we are not going to spend more time on the problem of many minds, then how about consciousness? We have seen John Searle's view that consciousness is important. But what might it be for? Can it influence our intelligent functioning in the world?

There is no doubt that being conscious is fun. In fact, it is difficult to see how we could extract any enjoyment from anything we do unless we are aware of our actions. Equally, being unconscious of what we are doing allows us to get away with bad or dangerous acts. We are seen as not being in control of ourselves. Is the essence of consciousness, then, control over our reflex actions? Without consciousness would we be human? Or merely another group of nerve cells trying to scratch a living?

How might we investigate consciousness? We have only

one tool available to us – the conscious mind. Ask someone what they are thinking about, and you will probably get a fairly civil answer. Depending on how well they know you, it could also be a detailed and illuminating glimpse of what goes on in their heads. Say we had a series of these conversations, ranging over a wide spectrum of subjects. Would we on that basis feel justified in saying we understood the other person, perhaps better than they themselves did? Sigmund Freud for one certainly thought so.

Freud began his investigations into the nature of the mind at a time when hardly anyone believed that there was such a thing as the *un*conscious. Most of previous philosophizing about the mind had emphasized the importance of consciousness. Introspection was a gift given to all. Everyone had access to their internal mental states. They knew what their minds were up to. What Freud proposed was that everyone had been mistaken. There were great tracts of the mind that were simply inaccessible to an individual. And in those caverns were many things that we would rather did not get out. These repressions were the cause of much mental illness and unhappiness. Freud's thesis was that by making them accessible – conscious – their malignancy could be reduced. Part of the reason that Freud's ideas caused so much trouble was that he was proposing that it was possible for someone else to know us better than we know ourselves. Freudian psychology turned out to have many flaws, although it still appears to be of value in certain cases.

But some, especially the philosopher Daniel Dennett, have pointed out that Freud's influence extended well beyond the confines of the consulting room. By changing our perceptions of our own minds to include the idea that there are areas of them to which we cannot have access, Freud laid a foundation for much subsequent psychological philosophizing. The gist of this is that minds are built up from smaller sub-units, themselves not minds. The sub-units come complete with the jargon of communications and computer science: they send messages back and forth, they call for information, they ask for help, and so on.

On this view – similar to Marvin Minsky's, as we have seen earlier – complicated minds are nothing more than assemblages of uncomplicated neural components. The mind is once again an emergent property of the brain. Dennett finds this view problematic:

> What is consciousness *for* if perfectly unconscious, indeed subject-less information processing is in principle capable of achieving all the ends for which conscious minds were supposed to exist? If theories of cognitive psychology can be true of us, they could also be true of zombies, or robots, and the theories seem to have no way of distinguishing us. How could any amount of mere subject-less information processing (of the sort we have recently discovered to go on in us) add up to or create that special feature with which it is so vividly contrasted?

There is a further problem. Whenever we perform some mental activity, such as speaking or adding up a list of numbers, there is a good deal of processing which goes on without our being aware of it. No amount of introspection can enable us to trace the steps that go on when we, for instance, compose a new sentence. It just happens. Are we then back to dualism? Is there some independent, ghostly entity inhabiting our machine-like brains?

There are two lines we can pursue here. The first is to ask how much of a brain we need to be conscious. The second is to follow Charles Darwin and ask what possible biological advantage consciousness could confer on us.

Is half a brain as good as one?

Remove a brain from the skull and you will see that it is made up of two almost identical halves. The hemispheres are in fact mirror images of each other. Linking them is a great bundle of millions of nerve fibres, called the corpus callosum. Around the middle of the nineteenth century, this mechanical observation prompted Gustav Fechner to consider where, if anywhere, consciousness might reside.

Fechner believed that brains cause minds. And he was determined to see whether the rational, objective methods of the physical sciences could be brought to bear on the seemingly intangible mysteries of the mind. The result was a new science called psychophysics – the application of physical principles to psychology. It is this hardnosed approach that makes Fechner's speculation so unusual. He wondered what would happen if the two halves of the brain were separated. Would one mind become two? Fechner himself was convinced that it would. He was equally convinced that the necessary experiments would never be performed. He should have been born in California . . .

It was known by the 1950s that cutting the corpus callosum seemed to make no obvious difference to the way the brain works – 'obvious' here being the important word. The knowledge prompted a surgeon to see if surgically splitting the nerve bundle could reduce the crippling effects of serious epilepsy. The operation was a remarkable success. The clinical importance of the operation, though, soon faded behind scientific insights gained from the study of the patients. For detailed investigation of their faculties revealed some astonishing changes.

Another peculiar fact about the brain is that each hemisphere controls principally the opposite side of the body. The corpus callosum appears to conduct information between the sides. The neuroscientist and Nobel laureate

Roger Sperry therefore set out to see what had happened to this ability of the hemispheres to communicate with each other. In a remarkable series of experiments, Sperry and his colleagues demonstrated that the two halves of the brain were to all intents and purposes independent. Each of them could take in information and process it without the other knowing what it was doing. The hands, in particular, seem to have minds of their own. But despite their apparent similarity, the two hemispheres do have different powers. The left is the seat of language. The right appears to possess visual skills – the ability to recognize, to draw, and so on. There is now mounting evidence that the picture is not so simple. Further investigation has shown that special talents can turn up in either the right hemisphere or the left. Split brains present a long and complex story.

For our purposes, the importance of this work is that it shows that minds may not be indivisible. Let us say that we meet someone whose left hemisphere never receives any information. That person would not then be able to talk to us, and we might conclude that they were unconscious – if we could not see them. The evidence of our eyes, though, tells us a different story. And if we communicate visually, we will find that the right hemisphere has plenty to put across. So although two hemispheres are better for complete human consciousness, there seems little doubt that one contains nearly as much. This finding seems to put one nail in the coffin of dualism. Mental things can no longer be thought of as indivisible.

Another comes from the social nature of consciousness.

The social mind

To return to another of our questions: the biological advantages of consciousness. Why should being conscious help animals to produce more young? If some form of biological necessity can be attached to consciousness, its mystery will disappear. The traditional scientific view is that conscious animals are simply more flexible. A conscious mind allows them to assess possible choices for their actions in a less rigid way than would a built-in, hard-wired system of nerves. This flexibility would aid them greatly in dealing with the changing world around them. The more flexible the animal is, the more chance it has of surviving, the more offspring it can produce. Eventually, the inflexible would die off, leaving those with consciousness selected for. QED. This is a nice, simple explanation. Many have pointed out, though, that the brain is vastly bigger than it need be. Many of the things it can do have no possible survival value. Mozart's powers would not have done him a lot of good in front of a sabre-tooth tiger, unless music really does soothe the savage beast. Some psychologists have therefore considered the social value of consciousness.

We will be looking in detail at the work of Dr Nicholas Humphrey on intelligence in Chapter 6. Briefly, he argues that the value of high intelligence is in allowing us to deal effectively with social interactions. Getting on with other people, predicting their actions, guessing their motives, finding a good mate and so on are, he says, about the most complicated things we ever have to deal with. It should therefore be no surprise that our brains have evolved great capacities to meet that challenge. His argument can be extended to consciousness. Imagine, he says, an animal that has everything it needs to get on in the world. It has sensory apparatus, limbs to move around on and grasp things, some form of information-processing and decision-making centre. But no consciousness, no 'inner eye' as Dr Humphrey puts it.

Now imagine another creature, identical in every way, except that this one does have consciousness, its inner eye allows it to look in upon the states of its mind and be aware of them. What would the practical consequence of this difference be?

> If we compare these two at a purely behavioural level the unconscious and the conscious animal might in most ways be indistinguishable. Both could be highly intelligent: both might show emotional behaviour, moods, passions, and so on. But while for the unconscious animal the behaviour would just happen as if its brain were effectively on auto-pilot, for the conscious one every intelligent action would be accompanied by the awareness of the thought processes involved, every perception by an accompanying sensation, every emotion by a feeling.

Suppose, argues Humphrey, that this is what consciousness amounts to. How would it affect our ability to operate intelligently in the world? Being conscious means that we can read our own minds: we know what it is like to be us. And knowing this, it becomes much easier to make sense of other human beings: 'We could, in effect, imagine what it's like to be them, because we know what it's like to be ourselves.'

Humphrey concludes:

> In evolutionary terms it must have been a major breakthrough. Imagine the biological benefits to the first of our ancestors that developed the ability to make realistic guesses about the inner life of his rivals: to be able to picture what another was thinking about, and planning to do next, to be able to read the minds of others by reading his own. The way was open to a new deal in human social relationships: sympathy, compassion, trust, treachery and double-crossing – the very things that make us human.

The value of consciousness, then, resides in enabling us to be social animals. That does not necessarily mean, by the way, that our brains have evolved in their particular fashion solely in order to enhance co-operation. As Richard Byrne and Andrew Whiten suggest, our higher intelligence may be of principal benefit in enabling us to manipulate and outwit others, the 'Machiavellian Intelligence', as they call it. Whether for co-operation or manipulation, however, such a facility quite clearly has survival value. Without it there would not have been any tribes, at peace or at war, eventually no nations, no culture, no tool-making, no agriculture. We would perhaps still be living a hunter-gatherer existence on the plains of Africa.

And what of the obvious objection: that not everyone's mind might work in the same way? Humphrey points out that it would be more of a surprise if they did not. We are, after all, descended from a common stock. We share the massive majority of our genetic make-up. It is far more likely that the basic processes operating in our minds are similar than that they are not.

There is an interesting piece of experimental evidence to support Dr Humphrey. The behavioural scientist Ronald Melzack reared dogs in total isolation from birth to maturity. They therefore learned nothing of 'natural psychology', of how to behave socially. Remarkably, the full-grown dogs seemed to have no understanding of pain. They would sniff repeatedly at a lighted match. The experience of being burned formed no lasting impression on them. Social experience, and Humphrey's inner eye, may have more than co-operation going for them.

Consciousness and multiple minds

There is an alternative explanation of consciousness – one that arises out of the several theories of multiple intelligence that we have already explored. It may be that the role of conscious experience is to weld together all the disparate minds inside our heads. To direct, arbitrate, cajole, encourage. In short, to rule. Marvin Minsky puts such a role thus:

> The important technical part of making a theory about multiple intelligences is trying to guess how the results of thinking in one part of the brain can be exploited by the others. So I think of these multiple intelligences as a little group which are working partly independently, but the beauty is that whenever one of them gets stuck it can get help from the others, and the top managerial procedures which decide that a certain interpretation, or a certain kind of thinking isn't working, and that another one should be engaged.
>
> So consciousness is really very thin. People think that they're aware of themselves, or that they know what they're doing, but when you probe it, the way Freud did, you discover that really you don't have any idea how you got an idea. When you make a sentence you have no sense of the grammar or how it was produced. That's why it takes scientists and generations of scientific work to find even the simplest principles of such things. So consciousness is sort of an illusion. As I see it, it's superficial formulations of what you're doing, and the top levels of the mind have very little insight into how all those other parts are working.

An illusion, or vitally important for our biological survival? At the moment, no one can tell.

5

SIMULATING
INTELLIGENCE

'I believe', writes Hans Moravec, author of *Mind Children*, 'that robots with human intelligence will be common within fifty years. By comparison, the best of today's machines have minds more like those of insects than humans.' Only a decade or so ago, futurologists were predicting that by the late 1980s or early 1990s we would be surrounded by Super Intelligent Machines. Those predictions were clearly wide of the mark. So what credence, if any, should we place on the idea that we will emerge in the early decades of the next century shoulder to shoulder with our artificial equals?

It's artificial but is it intelligent?

A classic experiment is being performed. The experimenter sits in a room in front of a desktop microcomputer, complete with visual display unit, and types in a series of questions. These are cunningly designed to elicit answers that will reveal the identities of two respondents located in another room, one a human being, the other a computer. If, at the end of the test, the interrogator cannot tell whether the answers are coming from man or machine, then the computer will have passed a milestone test that establishes its 'intelligence'.

Of course, the questions are not simply difficult mathematical sums. The computer can easily handle those, more easily than a human respondent. Indeed, if in the course of this test the computer were given a computation to perform that was clearly beyond the abilities of a mere mortal, it would have to make heavy weather of it deliberately. The machine would need to lie in order to protect its identity. So too would it lie if asked outright 'Are you human?', 'Does your family live with you?', 'Do you work in the city?' and so on.

To date no machine has successfully fooled an experimenter on this famous test, called the 'Turing Test' after the British mathematician Alan Turing, who devised it in the days when computing science was still in its infancy 50 years ago. And the reason is that no machine has yet been able to respond like a human to questions which require old-fashioned common sense, or which draw on resources of understanding, intuition and emotion. 'How do you feel about current AIDS propaganda?' 'Should women be ordained?' 'Should capital punishment be mandatory for terrorist murders?' Try these problems on a computer and you will soon see the limits of its grasp of human thinking processes.

The philosopher John Searle believes that no computer will ever transcend these limits. He contends that 'understanding' is very different in essence from working through some program, however elaborate this may be, and he illustrates this difference with the parable of what he calls the 'Chinese Room'. Imagine, says Searle, a computer programmed to translate a story given to it in Chinese. The computer has a huge, detailed program for finding the English equivalent of any Chinese character. It knows thegrammatical rules and structures of both languages and can move from one to the other with speed and facility. What it cannot do, argues Searle, is understand what it is doing. It is like having a group of workers, none of whom understands Chinese, handling counters with Chinese symbols written on them according to a book of instructions in English. By following the rules it is possible for the workers to produce translations from and into Chinese. But they still have no real understanding of the language. They are like individual electronic components in a computer. The Chinese Room in which they toil away is analogous to the computer itself.

Artificial intelligence and its limits

Not everyone agrees with the view that computers will never be capable of behaving in an 'intelligent' manner. In fact there are some who take a dramatically bullish attitude, contending that a program for cracking the Turing Test is not many years away and, when it arrives, as it inevitably must, it will open a floodgate. In the wake of a successful Turing experiment will come machines that are endowed with such emotive qualities as 'awareness' or 'happiness' and perhaps a few of the seven deadly sins! We will be returning to the implications of these predictions a little later, because they take us into some intriguing, if uncomfortable, areas of metaphysics. 'Can a machine have a mind/be conscious?' is perhaps the most provocative. So too is the converse 'Are human minds really only highly sophisticated machines?' With these issues we come up hard against the classic Mind –Body Problem that philosophers have wrestled with for centuries. Perhaps, through computer science, we may get closer to resolving it.

For the moment let us dwell on what computers can actually *do*. It is possible to compile quite an impressive list of achievements that take us close to intelligent behaviour as performed by humans. One area is in teaching. At the University of Illinois researchers have put together computerized teaching packages code-named PLATO and SOCRATES (short for Programmed Logic for Automatic Teaching Operations, and System for Organizing Content to Review and Teach Educational Subjects). The material to be taught is organized in small steps: until the student has correctly mastered one piece of information, he or she does not move on to the next. If a wrong answer is given the program loops back to an alternative route until the right responses are arrived at.

These programs offer two enormous advantages. First, the computers can take into account not just the current wrong answer but all a particular student's wrong answers, and come up with a 'diagnosis' of any general learning difficulty. Second, computers are tireless machines with near limitless capacity for handling information. They can teach one person or many, at elementary or university level. One leading computer scientist predicts that soon millions of students 'will have access to what Philip of Macedon's son Alexander enjoyed as a royal prerogative: the personal services of a tutor as well-informed and responsive as Aristotle'.

A second area in which the computer has made considerable strides in recent years is in playing chess. Now chess is a good model of high-level intellectual activity. Good players are often thought of as epitomizing what it is to be clever. Chess requires an excellent memory for gambits, moves and outcomes; strategic planning skills for seeing ahead and anticipating an opponent's game plan; an intuitive 'feel' for the current and future shape of the game and so on. At the highest level, chess depends very much on these strategic and intuitive elements rather than on the learning of moves pure and simple.

This is why, to date, the great chess players have been able to outplay computers. A computer, if large enough, could be programmed to take into account all the billions of possible combinations on the chess board, but when it comes to selection the relatively under-endowed human draws on skills that transcend those of the well-stocked machine. At least, this was the picture until recently; but the gap between human and machine is closing uncomfortably fast, as Professor Hans Berliner's research clearly shows.

At Carnegie Mellon University in Pittsburgh, Berliner – himself an excellent chess player with 20 years of experience in programming computers to make telling moves – has developed 'Hitech'. Like all chess-playing computers, Hi-tech has a wonderful memory. In a three-minute timespan it can take in the present state of a game and explore 30 million possibilities implicit in whatever move it might make next. In complicated situations it can certainly out-think the best players in the world by being able to hold in its silicon brain every possibility at once, whereas humans have to concentrate on a few at a time. All that in itself is impressive, but Hitech goes further than this. It has an inbuilt ability to evaluate the quality of any moves. And the machine estimates a high-quality move as one that embroils the opponent in high levels of complexity. 'What we want', says Hans Berliner,

> is to create situations where there are seven or eight plausible moves all the way down the line so that the game explodes at the rate of seven or eight possibilities per move, and nobody can follow that . . . Mikhail Tal of Russia, who was World Champion for a time, played this kind of chess and had a great deal of success with it. Very few people could beat him. He would beat them all, again and again, and in positions that later were found to be inferior, mainly because they couldn't handle the complexities of the situation.

Perhaps the best endorsement of the skill of Hitech comes from Britain's best woman player, Grandmaster Dr Jana Miles, who admits to being 'smashed flat' in the first two games she played with the machine. In the first game she reckons she lost because she did not take the computer seriously, other programs having failed to impress her. The second game, though, she did take very seriously, and she still lost: 'Its speed of calculation is phenomenal. It took all the material offered and it neutralized my attack very accurately and quickly, much faster than a player of acceptably high standard would do.'

Hans Berliner's machine chess player is still experimental, but he makes a confident prediction that, come the end of the 1990s, a computer program will be among the world's top ten players. He also adds that a computer that revels in complexity will not just prove its worth on the chess board.

'There are problems', he points out, 'that are combinatorially so complex such as chemical structures and various kinds of design problems that, if you have a machine which can even in a very rudimentary way explore the whole space of possibilities, it will find lots and lots of possibilities that nobody's ever thought of.' And that brings us to the third way in which machines are becoming more 'intelligent': in their ability to solve problems.

Problem-solving ability is often thought of as a measure of intelligence and creative thinking. Indeed, the psychologist Howard Gardner defines intelligences as 'a set of abilities to solve problems, or to fashion products, which are valued within society'. When one looks in detail at the process of problem-solving a common thread seems to be the ability to make useful connections. Thus, given a set of materials and the problem 'Build a structure to enable you to cross this river', you need to be able both to see how the materials themselves will interconnect and how they could be used to bridge the space between two river banks. You need, in solving problems, to try out ideas by assembling them mentally, evaluating alternatives, selecting solutions that fit best with the task. The same is true in purely abstract questions such as finding proofs in mathematics. You move from one point – the initial, given data – on to the next, then the next, by making a series of logical steps, selecting only those steps or transformations that bring the solution closer.

At the Massachusetts Institute of Technology, Thomas Evans devised a program for solving logical problems of the type that often figure in IQ tests. Whether or not these conform, by the way, to what Howard Gardner might term problems 'valued within society' is another question. The importance of Evans's program is the way it mimics the actual *process* of solving problems by humans, that of analogical reasoning. Here are some examples of Evans's problems. The question is: A is to B as C is to D1, D2, D3, D4 or D5?

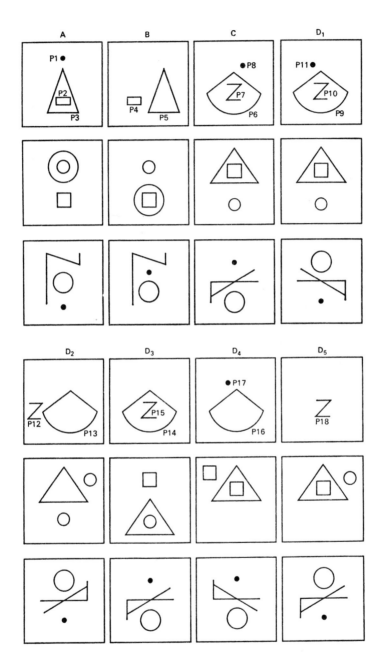

Faced with these three particular problems, by the way, the computer managed a score of 2 out of 3. It correctly chose D2 on the top line and D3 in the second line. But it failed in line three because here it is necessary to assess relationships between more than two objects or figures. Nevertheless, this computer program does exhibit a quasi-human capacity for assessing the relationship between two objects, then scanning among a list of possibles to find an analogue of that relationship in order to arrive at a correct answer: a basic feature of all problem-solving.

The intelligent robot

In an automated car plant there is not a human operative to be seen. Robot arms spot-weld body sections together; carry out engine part forging; spray paint the vehicles coming off the assembly line. These tireless automata never go on strike, need no rest breaks and do not care how hostile the environment is in which they are sent to work. It may be a dangerous nuclear reactor or a toxic chemical storeroom. Give them a task and they will perform it, endlessly and methodically. Already robots are being used extensively in a wide variety of industrial applications. It is an escalating field of advanced technology in the United States, Europe and Japan.

Yet today's robots are a long way from those human-like creatures that populate science fiction stories and films. No spot-welding robot has the thoughtfulness of Arthur C. Clarke's HAL in 2001. No paint-sprayer comes close to the puckish R2-D2 and C-3PO in *Star Wars*. Workhorses robots may be, but not loveable pets or wise confidants. At least, not yet.

According to Michael Brady, Professor of Information Engineering at Oxford University, there is no doubt that industrial robots of the current generation are limited. But he argues that they 'need to be intelligent'. It is not enough, he contends, to use the term 'robot' in the restricted sense proposed by the Robot Association of America: 'A robot is a reprogrammable multifunctional manipulator designed to move material, parts, tools or specialized devices, through variable programmed motions for the performance of a variety of tasks.' This is fine as far as it goes, but it fails to incorporate an important feature of any really useful industrial robot, namely, the ability to perceive what is going on in its immediate environment. It needs to be able to sense. Until it does the robot cannot react to the unexpected. Imagine, for example, a robot that carried on dutifully spot-welding when a human operator is standing in front of it. Or an assembly arm that made no allowances for changes in conveyor belt speed. There could be chaos or worse if the robot is not confined to a perfectly ordered, predetermined world – which is, of course, not the real world.

However, as Michael Brady points out, once equipped with quite simple sensing devices, a robot can become much more versatile. With more complicated sensing and gripping devices, any given robot could carry out even more applications and tolerate even more uncertainty. 'There is a price to be paid for versatility, however,' he writes, 'and it is (that) . . . the robot's model of the world needs to be more complex, and the robot needs to have a greater understanding of it. In short, the robot needs to be more intelligent.' A robot we might then define as a machine for making 'the intelligent connection of perception to action'. How far has research taken us towards realizing that definition?

Machines with senses
The ideal robot would be able to see, hear, feel, taste and smell. Its five senses would keep it in constant touch with a wide variety of environmental subtleties. It could then, like us, take appropriate action in response. Of all the senses,

by far the most powerful and complex is vision. A robot that could 'see' in much the same way as a human would be a remarkable machine indeed. Proper computer vision is proving extremely difficult and frustrating to develop. Take, for example, our ability to pick out patterns. Give a three-year-old child a picture of a farmyard and say 'Find me a tree', and instantly the finger will find the appropriate shape. Yet sophisticated programs running on multi-million-dollar supercomputers achieve comparatively poor performance on the very same task. Paradoxically, a five-dollar pocket calculator can outperform any human on computing tasks such as multiplying together ten-digit numbers. So what makes pattern recognition in particular and computer vision in general so different?

For one thing, even supercomputers may not be super enough for the magnitude of the data processing involved in computer vision. One component of this is 'edge detection' – the recognition of boundaries and overall forms. One advanced edge detector required 10,000 computer operations for each picture element, or pixel, that makes up the image. This means that 2500 million operations would be required on a simple image. A computer of moderate power might execute say, one, million operations a second. So it would take nearly three-quarters of an hour to process the input from one image, which is not exactly the instantaneous reaction you would need from a responsive robot.

However, several important research initiatives are under way to overcome the limitations of present machines. At Oxford University and at the Thinking Machines Corporation in Cambridge, Massachusetts, researchers are working on a technology that could bring a 40-minute edge filtering operation down to an impressive one-hundredth of a second. In various laboratories, too, work is going on to endow computers with an ability to recognize shapes and patterns not just in two dimensions, but in three. Again a leading centre in the field is the Thinking Machines Corporation, where the Connection Machine bodes well for real-time 3-D vision. To date we are some way off a machine that will generate perfect depth information in all situations, and even further from a processor as complex as the human brain, which contains a vast amount of inbuilt redundancy. Humans have not one but more than 20 processes for computing three-dimensional structure. Nevertheless, three-dimensional objects can now be recognized by machines, and soon Computer Aided Design (CAD) will include the facility for producing 3-D models automatically from images.

'Thinking robots'

'There is a widespread, though quite mistaken, view that the lower levels of control are quantitative, whereas higher levels are essentially qualitative.' Michael Brady argues that a simple robot arm with, say, an ability to put tops on beer bottles on a production line, is no different in its essence from a complex, all-seeing machine able to move on a collision-free path in unpredictable environments. 'Intelligence' is a matter of upgrading an unintelligent machine by giving it a more complex model or internal representation of the world in which it operates, together with an increased complexity in its data processing capacity.

As to how a machine should be built to achieve these levels of complexity, there is some debate. Brady believes that, although robotics is 'deeply linked to the study of human perception, cognition, and motor control', this does not mean that thinking machines need to be closely modelled on human beings. After all, planes fly with a different technique from that of birds. Why then should a robot hand, say, be a four-finger, one-thumb device, or artificially-driven legs have the same arrangement of joints as we have?

Consider, for example, attempts to build robots with 'bodily-kinaesthetic' abilities. No one would seriously suggest that 'Charlie', a table-tennis-playing robot being developed by John Knight and Dave Lowry, could attain the athletic prowess of an Ivan Lendl or a Florence Griffith Joyner. But that is not really the point. This ingenious vertical mast, about a metre tall, with a bat mounted on a little trolley, plays effective strokes by timing its shots and tracking the returning ball. It can, within its own world, solve its sporting problems and turn in reasonable performances.

On the other hand, most researchers into artificial intelligence acknowledge that it would be foolish to ignore the workings of the human brain when thinking about intelligent machines. Take the example of pattern recognition. One reason why this is so difficult for a computer is that it belongs to a class of problems known as 'random': that is, its solution requires knowledge of every possible state of a system – every possible variant on the pattern there is likely to be. The human brain is unique in its ability to solve random problems; thus, write Yaser Abu-Mostafa and Demetri Psaltis, 'many computer scientists and mathematicians have taken a closer look at how the brain works in the hope that the principles of its operation can be fruitfully applied in machines capable of solving random problems.'

From these observations of the brain have come computers built on the neural network principle; that is, machines consisting of a large number of simple processors – analogous to brain cells – extensively interconnected. At their laboratory in the California Institute of Technology, Abu-Mostafa and Psaltis have been experimenting with one such neural computer dedicated to pattern recognition. It is based on optical technology.

The basic idea is to arrange optical elements in the same way as neurones are arranged in the brain. On a conventional silicon chip there are limits to the number of electronic components that can be crammed together, determined by the fact that they are linked by wires. These wires must be separated by a minimum critical distance, otherwise the electrical signals they carry will interfere with each other. The two Caltech researchers therefore looked for another technology that does not suffer from this data communication drawback. They were given a clue by the functioning of the human eye. The eye lens takes light from millions of points in the pupil and redistributes it to millions of sensors in the retina. 'It is in this sense that the lens can be thought of as a highly capable interconnection device: light from every point at the pupil is "connected" to every point in the image focused on the retina.' Light beams, they reasoned, would make an interesting way to shuttle messages as nerve cells do in the brain. Beams can pass through prisms or lenses and still remain separate. And unlike electrical currents in a wire, light beams can cross over each other without mutual interference.

From these basic thoughts they moved on to develop their pattern recognition system, establishing their optical connections not through lenses but holograms. A one-inch-square hologram gives them the ability to interconnect each of 10,000 light sources with each of 10,000 light sensors: a facility that would be extremely difficult to accomplish on a silicon chip. In this way they move a step closer to the densely elaborate interconnective properties of human nerve cells.

Like brain cells, the optical 'neurones' work in a collective manner. The operation – or 'firing' – of one individual unit results in the sophisticated function of the neural network in total. Thus thousands of units collectively and simultaneously influence the state of one optical neurone according to the application of simple rules. It also allows information to be encoded in the neural connections themselves, rather than in some separate memory elements: each piece of stored information can be represented – as in the brain – by a unique pattern of neuronal connections.

All this amounts to a machine that is not dissimilar from a human brain. Just as a child learns to speak not by learning grammatical rules, but by imitation of structures in particular circumstances, so an optical computer can 'learn' various tasks. The programmer provides enough training data to allow the computer to set up its unique pattern of connections for each solution. Take, for example, the task of pattern recognition: specifically of getting the machine to recognize a tree.

'One would provide images of trees as training, allowing a specific pattern of interconnections among the computer's processing elements to be "imprinted" for each training image.' Although Abu-Mostafa and Psaltis admit that there are still a number of tough challenges to be met before optical hardware, arranged in neural architecture, will drive practical computers for dealing with difficult tasks such as pattern recognition, there are more than a few signs that such a technology does have a strong future. It will enable computers to tackle tasks beyond the reach of purely electronic methods.

The mortgage network

At the offices of Nestor Inc in Providence, Rhode Island, Dr Douglas Riley and his colleagues have been working on making a neural net perform something we usually associate with grey-suited bank managers. Their net is learning to decide who is likely to default on a mortgage, and who will be a good risk. The problem is complicated. The underwriters have a mass of data about the lifestyle, age, geographical location, family, employment and so on of their customers. From these they can make a reasonably informed decision about whether the loan will be repaid. They are, however, in a dilemma. To be absolutely sure that no loan is ever in default, the underwriters should be conservative – reject any application that looks even slightly suspect. But they would then probably also reject a number that would turn out to be perfectly good, and so the business would lose the commission on the loan. The underwriters therefore have a set of guidelines which allow them to process applications to an acceptable degree of risk.

The Nestor neural net has several thousand nodes. Interestingly, it is not composed of just one net. Mirroring theories of multiple intelligences, it is made up of several independent nets. The output of each of these is collated by a central overseer. The output of the overseer constitutes the net's decision. To train it, Dr Riley presented it with a set of information about loans gleaned from past applications. These data obviously contain some applicants who are good risks, and some who are bad. The network is set up to extract significant patterns from this information. The result is that it learns to embody the collective wisdom of the group of underwriters who processed the original applications. After training, the Nestor net can process several thousand mortgage requests in about half an hour.

Successfully? Here is the interesting part. It turns out to be quite easy to train the machine to mimic exactly the predictions of human underwriters. And it is possible to manipulate the conservatism of the net. So the human supervisor can instruct it to be extremely cautious in its decisions – to the extent, in fact, that none of its loans will ever default. Its predictions then agree with about 35 to 40 per cent of the underwriters'. On the other hand, the net can be told to take a few risks. It can then get as close as 90 to 95 per cent of the decisions made by people. And who sets the level of risk? 'We like to keep the humans in the loop,' says Riley. One intriguing prospect that he is now working on is to train the machine to make better predictions than people can. The way to do this is to review the quality of decisions made about loans in the past. So take a data set made up of loans granted three years ago. See how many of those have defaulted. Train the neural net with the three-year-old data. Then let it see what really happened to each of the mortgages. Re-train it in the light of that experience. The net will extract a pattern – perhaps one of which the human underwriters were unaware. It should then be better able to predict the fate of a particular loan. This research is at present in the early stages. But Dr Riley can already predict the outcome in borderline cases with much better accuracy than, as he says, flipping a coin.

At this point it is hard to judge how close neural networking might get to genuine artificial intelligence. But with the brain-based method of interconnecting elements we are already quite a long way from the idiot computers with which most of us are familiar nowadays. Here, potentially, is a machine that can learn from 'experience', that can adapt to input by reorganizing its internal representations. Here is, potentially, a machine with something approaching a real brain.

'Neural Darwinism'

In the Neurosciences Institute in New York, Professor Gerald Edelman and Dr George Reekie are working along the same kind of lines, again developing a truly adaptive artificial system modelled on the human brain. They reason that evolution provides animals with brains in which not all the fine detail is predetermined; there is plasticity and elasticity in the way it can operate, unlike the average, firmly preset computer program. The nervous system – the brain – has to interact with the world and through experience acquire the kinds of attributes that will enable it to function.

Those functions are not hard-wired at birth. We pick them up through learning.

Thus, Reekie and Edelman have built a machine that is a little like a developing child – not quite a blank slate on which everything has to be written by experience, but then again not highly specialized for a multiplicity of functions. Like an organism that perishes or survives according to its adaptiveness to the environment, this machine, in a limited way, operates in a quasi-Darwinian fashion. A machine codenamed Darwin Three is an automaton with a visual sense, a sense of touch and a kinaesthetic sense, knowing where its 'muscles' are. The machine is shown objects of different shapes on which it has to make a judgement based on the concept of categorization – 'good' or 'bad'. If it judges an object to be bad it rejects it; if good, it will reach towards it and try to grasp it. Like an animal in the world looking for objects that might be edible and tasting them, Darwin Three has to reach a simple decision as to whether something has value or not in its limited world. It has no previous information saying, for example, that round objects are desirable and square ones are not. It has to make up its own mind based on how well the object fits into its world or not, as the case may be.

'We believe,' says Reekie, 'that these very simple things that animals do in the wild are the most basic things the nervous system has to contend with . . . They are the things that computers today are the worst at doing, and we believe that once we understand how animals do those basic things, then all the more complicated things that only humans can do can be studied.' Compared to the human brain, with its vast numbers of interconnecting neurones, Darwin Three looks primitive, with only around 600,000 connections. But Reekie and Edelman's experiments do suggest that a machine can be built with quasi-human adaptability to its environment, without being totally preprogrammed in the first instance. It can learn to do useful things. It has then, in some crucial way, a form of basic intelligence.

Electronic expertise: the computer as consultant

Before we examine the implications of the neural computer – especially its 'adaptive' qualities – there is another field in which machines can display some of the mental skills that qualify as intelligent. This is the area of the so-called expert system. 'A widely recognized goal of artificial intelligence (AI),' says Dr Ronald Brackman, head of AT & T's Artificial Intelligence Research Department, 'is the creation of artefacts that can emulate humans in their ability to reason symbolically, as exemplified in typical AI domains such as planning, natural language understanding, diagnosis and tutoring.' For some years now, researchers in various laboratories have been working towards these goals by devising computer systems with two major elements: a huge knowledge base and the ability to reason with it for specific tasks. These expert systems have also been the focus of a good deal of commercial interest. In their drive towards the so-called Fifth Generation supercomputers for example, the Japanese put expert systems among the major applications for the technology of the 21st century.

An expert system is a computerized, knowledge-based system that behaves like a human expert. It has specialist knowledge of a particular field which it can apply in various ways. Now, expert systems are designed to operate not like cold, logical, sequential machines, but like human experts. That is, they use their vast store of knowledge to take short cuts, make inferences and deductions, jump from one possible solution to another and so on. Think, say, of a doctor making a diagnosis. He or she is presented with a patient displaying one or a number of certain common symptoms – headache, fever, upset stomach and so on – which could be indicative of literally hundreds of medical conditions or diseases. Progressively a diagnosis is arrived at. Sometimes the doctor might work analogically ('I've seen something like this before'); a number of tests might be performed; a hunch may be indulged. At all times a possible diagnosis – a solution to the problem – has to be checked against the medical knowledge base. If there is mismatch the diagnosis must be off-target.

In the display of expertise humans tend to use a number of heuristic rules, that is, empirical principles extracted through trial and error rather than through cold, scientific demonstration. In a computer chemical plant highly skilled operators develop a 'feel' for a process that is going awry, based on a few key observations. There is, in short, a certain fuzziness in the way an expert operates. It is this that computerized expert systems are designed to emulate.

Stage one in their design is to accumulate the expert's knowledge base, which is not the same as saying that the computer should simply be fed vast quantities of raw data. Having knowledge is to possess organized, useful facts which can readily be drawn on and applied. It is no use for a doctor, for example, to know all there is to know about each part of the human body if he or she lacks knowledge about how these facts interrelate. You cannot properly reason, deduce or infer without a framework or structure on which to hang individual items of information. You do not become articulate simply by learning all the words in the dictionary parrot-fashion, but by applying that vocabulary correctly and tellingly in the appropriate situation. In the same way, an expert's knowledge base has to be both systematized and flexible, able to adapt to any circumstances or problem with which it might be confronted.

This means that, in the second stage of designing an expert system, an ability to cope with uncertainty is required. Think again of a doctor, a human expert in treating disease. Rarely is a doctor faced with a straightforward task in diagnosing illness according to symptoms. A headache or nausea can indicate any of a number of illnesses. There is usually no automatic choice of diagnosis or treatment, because tests and symptoms only support a course of action: they do not dictate it. Thus to mimic the mental processes of a doctor, a machine would have to combine and weigh a number of possibilities before making a final assessment. Such systems do exist. MYCIN is designed to interact with a human expert, asking for information and suggesting treatments. MYCIN's speciality is the infectious nature of micro-organisms – about a hundred of them – and how to decide which of these is causing symptoms. Built into its program are certain 'probability factors' that allow it to weigh up the medical evidence and examine the validity of any con-clusions it might draw, very like a human pondering the pros and cons before opting for a particular course of action. Another medical expert system, CADUCEUS, holds knowl-edge of more than 500 diseases and 3500 signs, symptoms and test results. It can think through a problem, again like a human, starting from, say, symptoms and progressively narrowing down the possibilities until arriving at a diagnosis. In other fields systems have been developed for geological prospecting, helping here to guide the choice of sites at which to sink oil wells, again by working through possibilities and probabilities.

Artificial Intelligence: the shape of brains to come?

Throughout this chapter we have made no outrageous claims for the achievements of AI. All we are seeing at present are the first steps of an infant technology; a few signs of promise and some interesting pieces of work that will probably have a pay-off somewhere along the line. When and how is a matter for speculation. But there is no harm in indulging in a little thought experiment.

Instead of today's clumsy or monotonous industrial robots, there could come a time when an all-seeing, all-manipulating machine might perform the most delicate of microsurgery, say, to repair a damaged human brain. That would be a rare irony. Once machines have achieved a high level of adaptability they might, like humans, begin not just to respond to their environment but to master it. One of their first tasks would be to learn to make improved copies of themselves. And who can predict what the interaction between an intelligent machine and a human being might be? What kinds of art, science, love and hate might the toing and froing between living organism and living machine generate?

If you find the idea of a man–machine love affair distasteful, that would be understandable. But do not dismiss the idea as totally absurd. If human beings can develop a powerful affection for species other than their own, and generate romantic attachments to television icons in soap operas, it is not beyond the realms of possibility that a user-friendly robot could become companion and even soul mate. But, you may say, no one can convince you that any machine could appreciate a fine claret or respond to a Bartók string quartet. Yet how do we know? Intelligent behaviour – be it organizing a hunting party for a sabre-tooth tiger or revelling in urbane after-dinner conversation – means reacting to the world in a responsive, adaptable, creative way, being always ready for the myriad of novelties that it throws at us. Technically there seem no genuine obstacles, beyond that of degree, to making a machine (or a machine making one of its own) to achieve those ends. It is, in short, a matter of time.

Once we abandon the long-held but, as we have seen in the course of this book, unjustified belief in intelligence as some fixed, inner power – like some steady charge in a mental battery – and see it instead as a way of looking at the world, such predictions look reasonable. It has been possible for some time, of course, to build responsive machines. Think, for instance, of the thermostat in a central heating system, reacting to environmental variations – in this case temperature. The boiler does not dumbly go on pumping out heat when none is required, any more than we continue sweating in cold weather. This type of reactive machine is quite unlike a railway train or a food mixer which constantly has to be told what to do – go faster/slower, stop/start and so on. Even in these cases, though, the machine is not wholly out of touch with what is going on in the environment. A train has shock absorbers to monitor and respond to variations in the track surface. A food mixer's motor might have a cut-out device that automatically takes over in the event of overheating.

From the simple food mixer to a complex computer-controlled heating system, we can obviously see a difference in degree of adaptability. And it might go on up to yet another level. One can envisage the house of the future that monitors all environmental factors and automatically turns on or off lights, heating, humidity controls and air conditioning as changing conditions dictate. This total house might also welcome anyone entering a room; monitor its own fuel consumption (and adjust it in accordance with a predetermined budget); and provide atmosphere and mood in keeping with the time of day or season. Like Reekie and Edelman's Darwinian neural network, such a house would be preprogrammed up to a point. But beyond that it is on its own, adapting to the tasks that face it or the demands that challenge it. Within limits it can be said to possess at least one important feature of intelligence. The same can be said of many animals, in fact of a surprising variety of species, as we shall see in the next chapter.

6

THE DESCENT
OF MIND

What possible advantage in the evolutionary struggle for survival does intelligence confer on *Homo sapiens?* Does the ability to do differential calculus have anything at all to do with the number of offspring we might produce? Is intelligence, in the sense we have defined it, limited to human beings? Or might other animals possess it, to a greater or lesser degree?

Animals that can talk recur frequently in fiction. A bird that could speak appears to summon others to sing together in *The Arabian Nights.* Dr Doolittle gave rise to his own song – 'Talk to the Animals'. Animated films are full of talking and thinking horses, cats, in fact representatives of just about every species. The attractions of animal intelligence have great appeal, then, at least on a commonsense, emotional level. The philosopher John Searle has also pointed out another commonsense reason for believing that dogs, at least, are intelligent, even conscious: 'I just can't make sense of my dog's behaviour any other way,' he says.

At the same time, we seem unhappy about accepting the idea that animals have brain power. We believe that their responses to the outside world are simply reflexes, that they are merely living out some preprogrammed set of actions. Professor Herbert Simon, Nobel laureate, economist, and researcher into artificial intelligence, gives the example of a small bug wandering over the sea shore. At first, it appears to be tracing out a very complicated path. Perhaps it is looking for something, food or shelter. Or maybe it is tracking some fellow-bug. Either way, it appears to be 'intelligent'.

But on closer inspection, it becomes clear that the complexity of the animal's behaviour is forced upon it by the complex geography and topography of the beach. The ups and downs of the dunes force the creature to follow a particular path. There is no thought, conscious or otherwise, in operation here. No one would suggest that that bug is exhibiting intelligent behaviour.

Would we, though, think the same about a dog wandering the same shore? It is a paradox that we seem simultaneously able to hold and reject the notion that animals can be intelligent.

One reason for this might be our own notions of what constitutes intelligence which, as we have seen earlier, have some fundamental flaws. Cognitive scientists and psychologists are beginning to suggest that what we think of as highly intelligent behaviour – the ability to play chess, or to solve problems in calculus – are epiphenomenal. That is, they are at best the icing on the cake of normal thought, at worst the froth on our experience of life, of no real value to the nitty-gritty of biological survival.

They point out that most of the things that we take for granted, such as speaking, walking across the street, or interacting with a new group of people, all require massive amounts of brain power. On this view, we are all very nearly equal. Our heroes – the Beethovens, Einsteins, Picassos – are just like us, only more so. Psychologist Robert Weisberg, for instance, asserts that the thinking processes involved in ordinary, mundane tasks are exactly the same as those invoked by the most exalted intellectual activity.

If this view is right, then perhaps we have been applying the wrong tests to the animal kingdom. Perhaps it has made little sense to ask whether, for instance, apes can communicate in American sign language. Or whether chimpanzees can display great facility for tool-making. Perhaps we should be asking what would constitute intelligent behaviour on the animal's own terms.

It turns out that there has recently been a change in the attitude of many animal behaviourists. They now more or less accept as given that animals are smart. The fundamental question then is: how do we design tests which reveal that intelligence?

Calls of the wild

A dolphin is trained to perform underwater manoeuvres involving tool manipulation under the supervision of humans. The animal becomes a member of a team of oil-rig divers.

A chimpanzee is taught human sign language. The animal then teaches it to another. Both seem capable of recombining signs to form novel sentences.

A bee is able to adapt its behaviour to changing external circumstances, managing to find its way around as if it carried a map in its head.

Animals, other, that is, than our own species, are capable of many impressive feats. They demonstrate the capacity to communicate, to learn, to remember, to use simple tools, even to count in a rudimentary way. They may even be able to pool their intellectual resources to plan ahead, suggesting that they can handle the concept of 'the future'. Might it not be said that they display in a variety of ways behaviour that we could fairly deem intelligent?

After all, intelligence is at root nothing more than a certain style in relating to the world, a degree of adaptability that enables an organism to respond to and cope with novel and unforeseen demands. The age-old debate that surrounds animal intelligence is whether this adaptability – which many animals do indeed show to a high degree – is wholly preprogrammed and determined by the simple mechanism of stimulus and response, or whether it involves some degree of conscious mental activity. Do animals, in short, 'think' as we all understand the term?

Consciousness and self-consciousness

If animals can think, do they think about themselves thinking? If you look at yourself in a mirror you know that it is
you that stares back. You have a degree of self-consciousness.
Many people who come into intimate contact with animals,
such as pet owners, believe that their favourite dog or cat
similarly 'knows what it is doing'. As they sit by the fireside
and gaze into the animal's eyes they sense quite powerfully
that their pet is aware of itself and their relationship.
Performing dolphins, trained to carry out aquatic tricks,
will sometimes spontaneously squirt water at poolside
children with an apparent sense of mischievousness, while
trained chimps often behave like affectionate and sometimes spoilt children in their dealings with their human
keepers.

In what has become a classic experiment a psychologist,
Dr George Gallup, attempted to ascertain whether animals
have that sense of consciousness, and with it self-
consciousness, that anecdotal observation tends to suggest.
Gallup's subjects were chimpanzees. The animals were
given mirrors and allowed to familiarize themselves with
these novel objects. Then they were anaesthetized and
marked on their foreheads and ears with a bright dye. Now
if this procedure is adopted with chimps that are totally
unfamiliar with mirrors they pay no attention to their newly
acquired facial markings. But the chimps that had already
played with mirrors behaved quite differently. They looked
intently at these strange streaks of colour, reaching out for
them in an inquisitive manner. Just as we would in the
same circumstances – and unlike the chimps with no mirror
experience – the dyed animals recognized the image before
them as themselves, with interesting modifications. They,
like us, seem highly self-conscious. Oddly enough, this
finding only applies to chimpanzees. When Dr Gallup tried

the experiment with monkeys, gorillas and gibbons they seemed less 'self-conscious' than the chimps.

Concept handling

Clearly, intelligent behaviour includes an ability to handle concepts. Presented with a series of pictures of trees of different species – ash, oak, elm and so on – the young child can easily categorize these into the generic grouping 'tree'. Intelligent behaviour relies enormously on this capacity to classify and sift. Indeed, tests of this very capacity are standard in verbal reasoning exercises designed to determine IQ scores.

It turns out that other animals, too, can carry out similar conceptual processing. In a telling series of experiments, Dr Robert Herrnstein and his colleagues at Harvard University demonstrated that the humble pigeon is far from being a bird-brain. Using 35mm colour slides, Dr Herrnstein trained pigeons to peck at a disc whenever a slide contained, say, a tree or a flower. The birds managed to do this remarkably consistently, even when the target figure was partially obscured, or in silhouette, or when only a small fragment was shown. Once trained, the pigeons are very adept at discriminating objects and relating them to broad conceptual categories. Recently a group of researchers led by Dr Edward Wasserman at the University of Iowa have shown that the pigeon's conceptual qualities are more widely developed than even Herrnstein thought. Wasserman's experiments are designed to see whether pigeons can assign the objects they see to discrete conceptual categories, such as 'cat', or 'car'. The pigeons were shown 500 slides from each of four categories: cats, chairs, cars, and flowers. The slides were mixed randomly. Ten pictures from each category were used to teach the pigeons to recognize them. The rest of the slides were then shown. If the pigeon managed to place the new slide in the right category, it was given some food. If not, the next slide was shown.

Dr Wasserman claims that his pigeons placed about 70 per cent of the pictures in the right category. His view is that it is true conceptualization. Rote learning would not allow the pigeon to work out the right category for the unfamiliar slides. Also, intriguingly, the pigeons seemed to make no discrimination between 'natural' things – objects that they might have encountered in nature – and man-made ones. Pigeons, it seems, are not as dumb as we thought.

The same seems to be true of the parrot. Now parrots are well known for the ability to mimic mindlessly words taught to them by their owners. But the parrot's abilities go beyond that, according to Dr Irene Pepperberg of Purdue University in Indiana. Dr Pepperberg's African Grey called Alex can, if shown an object, correctly assign it to a shape or colour category. Thus shown a red square and asked 'What colour?' or 'What shape?' Alex will, more than eight times out of ten, give the correct answer.

Such examples of animal conceptualizers – and one could point as well to dolphins, chimps, even rats and bees – make us think again about the much-vaunted intellectual supremacy of humans. We are not alone in having some of the cognitive skills required for intelligent thought. Indeed, further research shows that animals often set about learning and recall in much the same way as we do (some even forget in a human-like fashion); that they have a concept of number; that they can represent the external world in their brain. This is not to say that among the clever dolphins at Sea World swims another Einstein or Plato, nor that chimps such as the celebrated Washoe use language in precisely the same way as we do. All that these investigations into animal thinking suggest is that there are fascinating parallels, and that any differences may be those of degree not kind.

In Amboseli National Park in Kenya, Dorothy Cheney,

Robert Seyfarth and Don Griffin – three well-known ethologists – witnessed an uncanny event that underscores this
point still further. A large herd of wildebeeste was grazing
in two groups when five lionesses approached. Two of the
lionesses climbed slowly, within full view of the wildebeeste,
to the summits of two adjacent mounds where they sat
down. Lioness number three slunk along the ground to a
point midway between the two groups of wildebeeste. Then
the fourth lioness rushed out from the trees behind one
group of wildebeeste and caused the startled animals to
gallop towards the other group out in the open. As they
dashed off, the third lioness that had taken cover seized one
luckless animal and smothered it. It became the meal of all
five lionesses.

There was such calculated precision about the whole
incident that it looked very like intentional, not haphazard,
co-operation. 'Why,' asks Don Griffin, 'should two lionesses
climb to conspicuous positions where the wildebeeste could
easily see that they presented no serious danger? Why should
a third sneak along the ditch to a position about midway between the two groups? Was it pure coincidence
that a fourth lioness just happened to rush out from
an optimal point at the forest edge to chase the wildebeeste over the ditch where one of her companions was
waiting?'

It is tempting to think that in this case the lionesses had
planned the whole campaign with military precision. If so,
this would mean not only that they were able to conceptual-
ize their tactics like footballers round a coach and to express
their cunning in a complex language. It would also mean
that they were able to project events mentally to some point
in the future; that they have a concept of time and can
communicate using 'tense'.

Distraction and disguise

The piping plover is a wading bird which has the misfortune to lay its eggs on sandy beaches. Although it employs camouflage for both itself and its nest, its young are vulnerable to a range of predators. The plover, though, has developed a cunning method for preventing its nest being ravaged and its young carried off.

What happens is that the plover becomes aware of the predator when it is still far away. The bird will then leave its nest, and move cautiously to distance itself from the eggs. It will begin to pipe with its distinctive song, then fly or walk quickly in any direction except towards the nest.

This behaviour is unusual. If startled while foraging, or when there are no eggs to protect, the plover will fly away as quickly as possible. It will also do everything possible to make itself inconspicuous.

The bird will then indulge in a series of tactics seemingly aimed at confusing the predator. It will make loud noises. It will run in a peculiar way. But the most dramatic action is what has been called the 'broken-wing display'. In this display, the bird will hold its tail or a wing in such a way as to make it appear to be broken. It will feign muscular weakness by running a short distance, and then apparently collapsing exhausted to the ground. These actions seem aimed deliberately at exploiting the predator's sensitivity to abnormalities in its prey – every hunter wants to come across helpless prey.

Here, though, the bird is not helpless. If the predator comes closer, the plover will retreat. If the predator loses interest, the plover will attempt to attract its attention again. The game plan is clearly to lead the predator away from the nest so that the eggs are safe, but without itself getting caught. Once the hunter has been led far enough astray, the plover will fly off, circle back, and land close, but not too close, to the nest.

This is a very complicated set of actions. At every step, the plover has to evaluate the consequences of its previous actions, and assess the likely results of its next set. If it gets any closer to the predator will it get caught, for instance? Has it moved far enough away from the nest to ensure safety for the eggs? Can it afford to stay away any longer when there might be other threats?

Traditionally, it has been thought that the plover is playing out an inbuilt, reflex programme, triggered by the approach of the predator. In this view, the bird is caught on the horns of a dilemma. Should it attack the predator, even though it then risks its own life? Or should it get out while the going is good? This conflict is supposed to generate confusion in the bird, resulting in random, almost convulsive, movement. Some have even suggested that the birds become effectively paralysed. Donald Griffin, one of the most distinguished animal behaviourists, has a robust response to this view:

> Anyone who has carefully watched the predator-distraction display of a small plover will find the concept of a paralytic convulsion quite difficult to reconcile with what he sees. The bird is clearly controlling its behaviour and modifying it in detail according to what the intruder does. It looks frequently at the intruder, continues in one direction if the intruder follows, but flies in a well-co-ordinated fashion back to the intruder's vicinity if he does not . . . There are many well-orchestrated complexities to the behaviour, and its adjustment to circumstances strongly suggests intentional reaction to the situation rather than crippling confusion.

Griffin goes on to point out that there are many subtleties and variations to be found in this sort of behaviour. He concludes that the birds must have some understanding of what they are doing, and of what the outcome is likely to be. In other words, they are experiencing thoughts, no matter how rudimentary they might be.

Dr Carolyn Ristau of Rockefeller University in New York has recently sought to illuminate the thinking processes of the plover further.

She was concerned to see whether the birds possessed any of the attributes she had come to regard as embodying 'intelligence'. One of these is a sense of purpose. Does the animal seem as though it is doing whatever it is doing deliberately? Dr Ristau has a number of criteria that allow her to judge whether plovers have purposes.

Firstly, does the plover try to behave in a way that will get the intruder to move *away* from the nest? Secondly, does the plover itself appear to know what it is doing? Thirdly, can it overcome obstacles – if it can be thwarted, and nevertheless achieve the goal, that would seem purposeful. Finally, Dr Ristau's view is that an animal that appears purposeful in one area probably is in another.

Dr Ristau's experiments were, as she says, 'masochistically fun'. She first built a remote-controlled mechanical racoon called, appropriately, Rocky. Although pretty nasty to plovers, Rocky was not too successful on the beach: he kept getting bogged down in the sand (illustrating perhaps the problems of extracting intelligent behaviour from machines). Dr Ristau then engaged the help of some human predators. The humans would approach the nest. The birds would always behave in such a way as to lead them away from it.

Dr Ristau's second criterion – monitoring – presented more experimental problems. Plovers have eyes placed on the sides of their heads, so they can spot an intruder approaching from almost any direction. How then was Dr Ristau to be sure that the birds were watching her specifically, and not some other threat on the horizon? The answer was to exploit the bird's blind spot. They cannot see directly behind them. The trick then is to approach from behind, but acting in such a way that the bird's attention is eventually attracted. If the bird swivels to track you, then you are fairly sure that you are the object of attention. Dr Ristau's plovers did exactly this.

How about overcoming obstacles, then? To test this, Dr Ristau's intruders ignored everything the displaying bird did – they did not follow it away from the nest. Instead of breathing a sigh of relief that it was getting away, most birds went after the intruder and tried to engage its attention. That, says Dr Ristau, 'begins to fill out a notion of purpose of behaviour'. Dr Ristau then wondered if the birds would react differently if they knew that the intruders had spotted them. She asked a group of students to dress up in different costumes and wigs so that they all looked different from each other, and from the scientists observing the scene. They would then walk past the nest at a considerable distance, about twenty or so metres. In one case they would scan the dunes where the nest was located. In the other they would ignore it. And indeed the birds did respond differently. If the intruder was looking towards the nest, the bird would get off it, and stay off it longer. They then looked to see if the birds could learn whether a particular intruder was dangerous, or posed no threat. Clearly, it does the bird no good to distract something that means no harm when there could be a really dangerous animal about. Again they had two differently dressed people walk past the nests. One of them just walked past looking straight ahead. But the other would walk close to the nest and hover over it. After a pause, the two intruders would again walk past the nest at a distance. The birds ignored the first one, but the one which had approached the nest earlier provoked a strong response.

This seems to suggest strongly that the birds can learn

very quickly, and can use their behaviour in a strategic way – they can turn it on and off when appropriate.

It has been suggested that the evolution by natural selection of these behaviour patterns as unthinking reflexes is sufficient to account for their existence, in the sense that birds that possessed them would have more offspring. It is difficult to see, though, how reflex can account for the richness of the animal's strategy for dealing with threats. Ristau's study of the plover is just one of a number of studies indicating that animals are much smarter than we think. Others have looked at hunting tactics adopted by groups of lions, and at those adopted by their prey in order to avoid being eaten. The experiments of Gallup appear to demonstrate that chimpanzees have self-consciousness.

Closer to home, the antics of pets often suggest that they know a great deal about their owners, and how to manipulate them. Domestic cats lead a life of fairly unremitting luxury. Food arrives regularly. Stroking is administered. In short very little disturbs the comfortable daily routine, and the cat displays rather little interest in the people around her. Occasionally, however, the owner will become distracted by other concerns. The odd howl will be ignored. Eventually the cat decides that something more dramatic is needed. She will then regress to the sorts of things she did as a kitten, nearly 15 years ago. She will roll over on her back and purr. She can even be tempted to chase a piece of cotton. In no time, she is again the centre of attention. Again, it is possible to argue that this is just reflex – one set of stimuli did not work, so she tried another. John Searle's argument, though, is persuasive. It is impossible to make sense of the cat's behaviour without the assumption that she is at least dimly aware of her actions, because she will sometimes do the same thing apparently just for the fun of it. Warm, well-fed, and well-stroked, she will sometimes put on a show of kittenish charm. It is hard to see how two opposite stimuli can produce the same response, unless she is able to manipulate her own behaviour.

There is further evidence from the efforts of some animals to manipulate their environment. Birds' nests are perhaps the most familiar of these, but there are many other examples. The larvae of caddis flies, for instance, will cover themselves with accretions of sand, leaves and other matter. It might seem that caddis flies can't be choosers – that they would make use of anything that floats past. In fact, the various species display considerable discrimination in choosing their building materials. They seem to do this by assessing the materials with their mouths, rejecting those that do not appeal. Again, it is easy to speculate that the caddis fly is a slave to its genes. But the list of genetic instructions that would account for this master builder's abilities is a very long one indeed. A far simpler insight into the behaviour is to suppose that the larvae know what they are doing at some level, and that their behaviour is purposeful and directed.

Once ethologists had started to reconsider the behaviour of even simple creatures in these terms, they began to find examples of intelligence almost everywhere they looked. They have catalogued a large number: wasp, ant and bird nest-building; the use of tools by ant-lions, crabs and mammals, including chimpanzees; dam-building by beavers, a feat of civil engineering; and, perhaps most interesting, the communication abilities shown not only by higher primates but by ants and bees, who use a complicated dance to tell other bees the direction and distance of a food source.

The Dance of the Bees

Several decades ago, the Austrian ethologist Karl von Frisch became interested in the strange dance performed by honeybees as they returned to the hive after scouting, presumably for food. The bee, attended by several other workers, traces

out a figure of eight on the surface of the honeycomb. The
attendant bees press their heads and antennae to the scout's
body. As the scout traverses the straight portion of the figure
of eight, she moves her abdomen vigorously from side
to side, a movement which gives the dance its name –
Schwanzeltanz, or waggle-dance. The returning bee also
gives off odours which stimulate the other workers.

It turns out that the dance signals the direction and
distance of a new food source. Remarkably, it seems only
to be performed when the food is of a type needed by the
colony – any old edible thing will not do. This strongly
suggests that the dance is part of a complex system of
communication operating throughout the hive so that every
bee that needs to know can find out what is going on in,
say, the food supply.

The orienteering part of the dance comes from the direction of the straight line portion. If it is straight up the
honeycomb, the food can be found in the same direction
as the sun. As the orientation of the line changes on the
face of the comb, it represents different directions with
respect to the sun. On cloudy days, the bees can use the
patterns of polarized light produced in the sky by the diffused
sunlight. The distance of the food is indicated by the speed
of waggle – slow for near food, faster for further away. The
fervour with which the bee dances also seems to signal the
quality of the food source. The local equivalent of Harrods
Food Halls induces dervish-like enthusiasm. There are
many other aspects of the dance, and several questions are
posed. How can the attendant bees interpret the dance in
the darkness inside the hive? Does the dance compensate
for the movement of the sun in the time taken for the scout
to return to the hive? And so on. Nevertheless, it appears
unquestionable that information is being imparted by the
use of symbols. The attendant bees can usually find the food
source after seeing the dance.

Another use of the dance occurs when the bees are forced to find a new home. In the 1950s, Martin Lindauer conducted a series of experiments in which he forced a swarm of bees to choose a new hive from among a number of more or less desirable locations. Again, scouts went out. Those that found something suitable performed the dance on their return. Again, the dance indicated direction, and the energy put into it reflected the bee's assessment of the desirability of the new home. The effect of this dance is to recruit other scouts. They visit over a period of days those sites suggested by the most vigorous dances. When they return to the swarm, they too perform a dance. The result is that a sort of bee-consensus gradually emerges. Eventually, all the dances indicate only one likely home.

What is remarkable about this sequence of events is that it involves a profound change of mind among some, if not most, of the bees. In fact, the bees seem remarkably willing to change their 'minds'. Lindauer marked some and then watched them over a series of dances. He found that those that had found less suitable niches would stop in the middle of their dance, and watch a different, more vigorous dance. The newly educated bees would then take off to visit the home indicated by the different dance. On their return, they would also begin dancing about it, this time with increased enthusiasm.

The conclusion seems inescapable. Scouting bees do not only impart information to their fellow bees as a matter of reflex. They are also aware of the communications of other bees, and will modify their behaviour on the basis of this information. This is a powerful and flexible way to get information across. The dance of the bees is an example of other animals using a form of language to cement their societies together. Might there be others?

Apes that talk

In the 1960s, Alan and Beatrice Gardner came to an interesting conclusion about the abilities of apes. They were convinced that apes could communicate with one another –
observations of their interactions in the wild implied as
much. And they were also convinced that apes were intelligent. Why then had previous efforts to teach them language
failed? The Gardners reasoned that the apes were not too
unintelligent to learn, but that they lacked the physio-logical
ability. Their vocal tracts were simply not up to the job.
Their solution: use American Sign Language instead.

They embarked on a series of experiments with a chimp
called Washoe. Their approach was to rear the chimp almost
as if it was a dumb human baby. They signed to her, and
encouraged her to make her needs known by signing back.
The results were very encouraging. Washoe was able to
accumulate a vocabulary of more than 130 signs. She could
use these to identify objects correctly when shown their
pictures. She also showed a rudimentary ability to combine
signs to generate new ones – 'water-bird' for 'swan' being a
graphic example.

The Gardners' work stimulated others to follow. Among
the most noteworthy are David Premack's experiments, where
coloured plastic tokens are used to form questions. One
chimp, Sarah, could select the appropriate token in response.
Duane Rumbaugh and Sue Savage Rumbaugh have used a
keyboard on which the keys are illuminated. Their chimps
can select the right key to answer a question or to ask for
something. Two of the chimps have even learned to use the
keyboard to communicate with one another.

There do, however, remain doubts. At a basic level, some
critics are unconvinced that the apes are actually using
language. They advance the argument that the apes might
be doing nothing more than learning to produce a response

which will bring them reward. Their actions are no more accomplished than the salivation of Pavlov's dogs when presented with a ringing bell. The most important objection rests upon the apes' ability, or inability, to form novel concepts by combining elements of their vocabularies in new ways. Here, the results have been disappointing, 'water-bird' notwithstanding. At the same time, the research is in its infancy. New teaching techniques, or perhaps efforts on the parts of the researchers to learn the apes' own language, might yield better.

However, the majority of people who have conducted these studies or reviewed their significance are in no doubt that the apes have learned something about language. And as Descartes said: 'The word is the sole sign and certain mark of the presence of thought.' Just because animals are dumb does not mean that they are dumb.

We must also not forget that just about every animal species also possesses perceptual abilities. As we mentioned at the beginning of this chapter, many scientists are now beginning to think that the ability to see, to get around the world, to get on with your fellow creatures, are marks of intelligence.

The accumulating evidence, then, suggests that we must not patronize animals. They can deal with the world on their terms probably as well as we can on ours. And it is interesting to speculate what might be the animal equivalent of chess or mathematics. Possibly our conviction that we are the only ones with skills that do not seem directly related to survival is not well founded. As we come to understand better the way animals behave, it may be that we will come to uncover hidden applications for seemingly inexplicable or 'useless' qualities.

Into the minds of others

Psychologists have already thought about hidden utility for some human abilities. Instead of assuming that our gross

mental development was accidental, they went to work on
the hypothesis that it must be of some use to the survival of
the individual. There have been, of course, many attempts to
link intelligence directly with evolutionary success. Crudely,
the argument goes that the more intelligent – flexible – an
individual animal, the more able will it be to cope with the
slings and arrows of life. It will therefore survive longer, and
beget more offspring. In time, the children of intelligent
parents will come to dominate.

It is quite easy to see the strength of this argument applied
to the days when our ancestors roamed the plains keeping
away from hungry beasts. And indeed, the psychologist
Robert Sternberg points out that these sorts of survival skills
might still be important. Put, he says, kids from a ghetto
next to middle-class offspring. The ghetto kids often appear
stupid on any of our present measures. But put them down
in a hostile inner city, and the survival skills of the ghetto
come to the fore. The shortcomings of the middle-
class children can result in their becoming literally 'dead
meat'.

Leaving for the moment the question of heredity and
intelligence, this argument has a flaw. There is no evidence
that more intelligent animals have more descendants. The
population geneticist Professor Richard Lewontin gives the
example of post-war America. There was tremendous concern among the intelligentsia that the thick would inherit
the earth. The birth-rate among college leavers and high
achievers was falling, whereas among the less educated it
seemed to be rising. The concern itself provokes a certain
amount of distaste, but it was misplaced. The average
intelligence of the American population does not seem to
have declined – although there are suggestions that it is not
rising as fast as in, say, Japan.

Clever family planning

Although it may, as we have seen, be unwise to link the intelligence of an individual with his or her reproductive success, there may well be something in the argument that intelligence does confer family benefits. Imagine a fertile couple hunting and gathering thousands of years ago. They want offspring to help them in their labours and to maintain their line. But they do not want too many because, then as now, a large brood of children represents an unwelcome drain on domestic resources. Nor do they want too few, because that might ultimately lead to a dead end in the lineage. So they need to get the balance right.

Intelligence would be the means they would employ to get their family number just about right. As Paul Colinvaux, Professor of Zoology at Ohio State University, wrote in his readable book *Why Big Fierce Animals are Rare*, 'In operating their Darwinian breeding strategy people must always have been looking into the future. Sometimes their reasoning may have been clear and direct; learning from the Joneses, all of whose children starved one winter because there was not enough food to go round, and from the Robinsons who made it through with their more moderate brood.'

Hints and tips on what constitutes an optimum breeding pattern according to changing conditions may have been acquired from the elders of the community who passed on their hard-earned wisdom. The better one listened and learned and adapted one's lifestyle to meet the world's vicissitudes, the more successful one would be. Indeed, the same may still be true. We live on a planet that is rapidly being milked of its resources. We cannot afford to produce children solely in accordance with the philosophy of 'the more the merrier'. We too, in the technological twentieth century, a long way from the harsh landscapes of the plains over which our distant ancestors roamed, have to fine-tune our breeding patterns if we are to survive and flourish. Our intelligence enables us to understand the great environmental issues and come to a rational judgement. Whether or not we choose to exercise it is, of course, quite another matter.

However, although intelligence may be helpful in promoting the advantages of family planning, this is not its only merit for humankind. Indeed it may well be of secondary importance to another kind of advantage inherent in our adaptive, subtle minds. Not a biological asset but a social one.

Natural psychologists

Building on a suggestion by Dr Alison Jolly, the British scientist Dr Nicholas Humphrey argues that the reason we have developed such extensive mental capabilities is not to deal with the mechanics of the world, but with the other minds resident in it – our fellow human beings. Humphrey started his scientific life as an experimental psychologist, trying to unravel in detail the mechanisms in the brain which underlie human and animal behaviour. He found, though, that this reductionist approach was taking him further and further away from what he considered to be the important questions. In particular he was concerned to find out why minds have evolved to be the way they are. What purpose might they serve?

He began to gain some insight during a trip to observe mountain gorillas in Rwanda, where he had the opportunity to inspect and measure the skulls of some dead individuals. His observations impressed him with the size of the gorilla brain. Also, it showed differences in the size of the left and right halves, differences which in humans are implicated in the use of language. The conclusion was that gorillas are animals of high intelligence, capable of problem-solving of a high order.

Yet here Humphrey found another puzzle. The life of a gorilla in the wild is remarkably easy. There are no natural predators – apart of course from man – and food and shelter are close to hand. Where were there problems to be solved, difficulties to be overcome, that might require a large and well-developed brain? Humphrey reasoned that the problems must be invisible. By drawing on his own experience of what worried him, he came to understand that the most difficult questions facing the gorillas are social ones: how to deal with their fellow gorillas; how to weld together a cohesive social group; how to avoid strife by knowing what other gorillas might want, or were going to do. As he points out, these problems are not trivial. A dispute over a mate can provoke a fight almost to the death.

Humphrey concludes:

> The forest may not present any great problems to gorillas, but the behaviour of other gorillas can and does. The intelligence required to survive socially is something of quite a different order to that needed to cope with the material world. Social intelligence is clearly the key to the great apes' biological success. It is in dealing with each other that these animals have to think, remember, calculate, and weigh things up inside their heads. And social intelligence requires every ounce of brain power they have got.

The logical follow-up was: if gorillas spend their mental resources on understanding other gorillas, might not our human brains have developed for the same purpose?

By looking at discoveries then being made about the lives of our early ancestors millions of years ago, Humphrey became convinced that the key to the rapid expansion of the

early human population was that they could get along
socially. They could organize themselves to hunt, to find
shelter, to gather food. To make such groups work it was
essential that each member be sympathetic to the feelings
of others. Those who understood this best were most likely
to be successful socially, to attract mates, and to produce
offspring. Over time, these 'Natural Psychologists' would
come to dominate. Those who could not exist within society
would die out.

The argument is persuasive. We all experience difficulties
with our social lives. We are puzzled, angered, charmed,
by the behaviour of our relatives, enemies, friends. We seek
to understand their behaviour in terms of our own – a sort
of 'If I do this will my mother/father/sister/brother/girlfriend/
boyfriend object/be happy' form of anticipating and deflect-
ing problems. The key is introspection. If we have insight
into what drives us to certain actions, we have fairly good
reasons to believe that other people will respond in the same
way. For the most part they do, otherwise society would
collapse. And when we come across someone whose behaviour does not accord with our own internal models of what
is right and proper, we tend to reject them.

Humphrey puts it thus: 'It is as if I, like every other human
being, possess a kind of "inner eye" which looks in on my
brain and tells me why and how I'm acting in the way I am
– providing me with what amounts to a plain man's guide to
my own mind.' And he quotes Thomas Hobbes: 'Whosoever
looketh into himself and considereth what he does when he
does think, opine, reason, hope, fear &c. and upon what
grounds, he shall thereby read and know what are the
thoughts and passions of all other men upon the like oc-
casions.'

There are other subtleties. Humphrey's ideas require
consciousness to act as the vehicle for his plain man's guide,
a position some scientific psychologists find uncomfortable.

It also depends on every social animal having the ability to recognize its fellow-creatures. If it confused two that behaved differently, the results could be unpleasant. This sort of mechanism might, therefore, be restricted to animals with a rich social life. And the argument has it that these will have some form of self-consciousness. This seems fine for apes, even dogs. But what about the superbly orchestrated societies of ants and bees? There is increasing evidence supporting the view that even these small collections of nerve cells might know what they are about. In fact, Donald Griffin has argued that the limitations of an insect nervous system might make it important for them to have some way of knowing what other insects might do, without the necessity for a neurologically expensive, hard-wired reflex for every possible occurrence. 'While the six-legged natural psychologist may need only to distinguish with her millimetre-sized brain between a few categories of companion, rather than between twenty or thirty individually-known group members, her ability to do so may be of equal or greater importance. If conscious empathy is helpful in one case, it may be equally helpful, or more so, in the other.'

He also points out that our human concept of recognition as applying to the individuals around us might be inappropriate for insects. Insects might find it necessary to recognize only certain *classes* of other insects, because their behaviour is necessarily circumscribed. So an ant can know that a worker is likely to behave in a certain way at a certain stage of development, without being able mentally to pin a name on its forehead. 'It is as though one's social companions were sets of identical twins or triplets who responded in exactly the same way to one's advances, so that having selected the correct set, it did not matter whether one solicited attention from Tweedledum or Tweedledee.'

Programs of the mind

Another piece of corroborative evidence may come from the
mysterious 'landscapes of the night' that constitute our
dreams. According to the psychologist-cum-computer-
scientist Christopher Evans, there is probably good reason
for our spending about one and a half hours every night of
our lives in that fairly frenetic form of sleep known as REM
(Rapid Eye Movement). During REM sleep the brain seems
to switch to another gear. These are the periods when we
have our dreams. Evans elaborated a computer theory of
dreams that runs somewhat along these lines. During the
day the brain is busy being bombarded with sensory input,
experience and sensation but it cannot assimilate all this
while the brain-computer is still 'on-line'. REM phases are
when the mind slips off-line and processes that experience,
assimilating it perhaps into its astonishingly numerous array
of programs which then become updated.

Dreams, speculates Evans, may thus be a strategy for
survival. We need them in order to remain adapted to our
environment. For humans, of course, that environment is
essentially social, full of people we have met and are likely
to meet again soon. So dreams are, he writes, 'like dress
rehearsals for events we can expect, hope for or fear in
everyday life. Situations present themselves in which the
dreamer is an actor, playing a part, coping with the often
strange twists of the plot, keeping abreast of the unfolding
drama.' Then Evans makes the link with Nicholas
Humphrey's social interaction notion. 'We are, after all,
social creatures whose lives are highly coloured if not ruled
by personal relationships and situations. If indeed we are to
stay mentally and emotionally well-adjusted we have to
accommodate others . . .'

On closer inspection this connection looks more and
more attractive. The less mature we (and other animals) are,

the more time is spent in REM sleep. We need to dream more when we are young, perhaps to carry out the enormous amount of programming and reprogramming required for later life. With little direct experience of the outside world young children may need to 'prepare for the interactions to come by staging their own nightly series of internal dramas'. As we grow older this need diminishes because experience teaches us how to handle ourselves socially. Thus there is less need to rely on functions of the brain's own making, less need to model the behaviour of others, to be 'natural psychologists'.

We have seen in this chapter that we put ourselves on an undeserved pedestal. Despite centuries of anthropocentrism, of belief that we are somehow unique in our abilities, evidence is emerging that we were wrong. Ethologists have begun to uncover a richness of behaviour in their field of study that suggests we were wrong ever to cast the rest of the animal kingdom as unthinking automata, a view which goes back to René Descartes. Indeed, even Descartes' conviction that language and thought go hand in hand is now being turned against him. Animals do use symbolic communication, even though we may not understand what it means. No less a student of the human mind than Carl Jung was in no doubt about the importance of findings on animal communication. In 'Synchronicity, a causal connecting principle', he commented on Karl von Frisch's research:

> . . . bees not only tell their comrades, by means of a peculiar sort of dance, that they have found a feeding-place, but they also indicate its direction and distance, thus enabling beginners to fly to it directly. This kind of message is no different in principle from information conveyed by a human being. In the latter case we would certainly regard such behaviour as a conscious

and intentional act and can hardly imagine how anyone could prove in a court of law that it had taken place unconsciously . . . We are . . . faced with the fact that the ganglionic system apparently achieves exactly the same result as our cerebral cortex. Nor is there any proof that bees are unconscious.

That animals can think and have some sort of mental life, no matter how crude, now seems to be beyond doubt. Yet we are left with another question. What possible use can an ape have for the potential ability to learn American Sign Language? Here the answer may lie in expanding our restricted notions of evolutionary advantage. Not every threat in our own history has come with fangs, or threatened us with blizzards or hurricanes. Perhaps the most dangerous challenge to our individual survival has come from creatures of our own species. Ability to understand how they will behave demands great sophistication and power within our brains, for these social interactions are probably the most complex and changeable problems we will have to solve. In fact, they probably make playing chess or solving differential equations look like child's, or ape's, play. And what goes for us may well go for other species too.

7

SNAKES AND LADDERS

In the past decade or so, corporations the world over have woken up to a fact that educationalists have always known: that the most precious resource we have is not oil or gold or plutonium, but brains. No longer does a company measure its assets purely in terms of inanimate plant and machinery, or compute its profits solely in the language of the balance sheet. Nowadays, enlightened companies rightly include in their overall estimation of the firm's worth some notion of its human resources. Indeed, in some, the very phrase 'human resources' is ousting the impersonally bureaucratic term 'personnel'.

What is true for a company is also true of a nation. As the political scene changes, trading conditions fluctuate and international markets lurch from one condition to another, the responsiveness and adaptability of people to constant challenge and novelty become of paramount importance. A nation needs all the intellectual talent it can muster. For a long time the idea has persisted that this resource is fixed and therefore unalterable. But, just as we can now see that intelligence itself is far from being hard and fast, so too must we abandon the concept of a national mental endowment that is not amenable to improvement or enhancement. We should not think, either, that any changes can only be modest. Nor indeed that they will only be for the better.

Japan: Land of the Rising Sun (and Escalating IQ)

In 1982 a psychologist from the New University of Ulster in Coleraine, Northern Ireland, published a paper in the academic journal *Nature* with a title that typifies the restraint shown by that august publication: 'IQ in Japan and the United States shows a growing disparity'. Had that psychologist – Professor Richard Lynn – been asked to concoct a headline for a popular newspaper he might have offered something along the lines of 'Shocked Americans outsmarted by Japanese' or 'The Intellectual Overthrow of the West' or some such bombshell. Lynn's findings certainly were, and still are, extraordinary.

He had studied the performance of Japanese school-children on the well-known American IQ test 'WISC' – the Wechsler Intelligence Scale for Children – which had been revised and standardized to make it suitable for use in Japan. The WISC measures a variety of attributes such as spatial ability, memory span and numerical skill, and Lynn traced the results on all these over 25–30 years, from the period directly after the end of World War Two to the late 1960s.

Over the same period the average American IQ was around 100. At the beginning of the period Lynn analysed, the average Japanese IQ was 105. By the end it had risen six points to 111. Thus not only was there a demonstrable disparity between US and Japanese schoolchildren, but that gap, according to Lynn, was widening. As it happens, 111 seems to be the highest mean IQ of any nation. It outstrips other advanced Western countries too, including Britain, France, Germany, Australia and New Zealand. The benefit of this apparent intellectual superiority in the international arena is not hard to find. Lynn writes: 'The Japanese IQ advantage may have been a significant factor in Japan's outstandingly high rate of economic growth in the post–World War Two period.'

Within months of Lynn's provocative paper appearing in *Nature*, the same journal published a complementary research report from James Flynn of the University of Otago, in New Zealand. Flynn took issue with Lynn's results not because they showed a substantial rise in Japanese IQ scores, but because the gains were just not high enough. Flynn reckoned that they were even more impressive, not a 6-point rise but something around the 14- or 15-point mark: a truly staggering improvement over only a couple of decades. Now not everyone agreed with that estimate, including Lynn himself. A complicated debate ensued, charged with fine academic distinctions and labyrinthine statistical argument.

It could be that Flynn had overestimated, according to one observer, because he had placed too much weight on the so-called 'block design' sub-test in which children are given various coloured blocks to arrange in certain patterns. On this test alone the Japanese school population appears to have a mean IQ of the order of 140 – well into the band in which they could pick up university doctorates and other advanced degrees. It seems unlikely that *all* the Japanese are potential PhDs. Moreover, if the block design task is excluded from the comparative scores, the US and Japanese IQ differences are reduced to just a few points.

What causes the changes?

Whatever the true picture concerning both the alleged gap between Japanese IQ and that of the rest of the world, and the rate at which it seems to be growing, there seems little doubt that since World War Two something has happened in Japan to bring about marked improvements in intellectual performance. The question, of course, is: what?

In a radio interview shortly after the publication of his original findings Lynn was asked this very question. His response was as follows.

I think this would almost certainly not be a genetic increase. It's very difficult to see how there could be an increase of this magnitude arising from genetic causes over the course of one generation. Therefore, we go to the other broad line of explanation and suppose that this is an environmental increase. Well now, an obvious line of explanation could be to imagine that there was some sort of educational improvement in Japan. It is a very competitive educational system they have there, with very considerable parental pressure exerted on children to achieve intellectually. However, this looks very unlikely to be the environmental factor that is operating. The reason for that is that the full extent of the increase is present among five-year-olds. Therefore, this seems to rule out effects of the school. It seems to be something that is happening before the age of five. This would probably incline one to look at some sort of general improvement in nutrition. If you know that the Japanese suffered a degree of under-nutrition in the war and immediately after the war, then we know that the birth weight of Japanese babies has increased rather substantially from that generation to the present, the height of Japanese children in adolescence has increased. So, there's a lot of evidence to show that there has been a general improvement in the nutrition of the Japanese and I would think this is a fair candidate for the factor which might have been operating. (*BBC Radio 4, 31 May 1982, 'Science Now'*)

The idea that improved social and economic conditions – as exemplified by better standards of nutrition – can produce short-term jumps in performance on intelligence tests is certainly an attractive one. Japan has advanced from a rural, feudal society to an urban, industrial power in a few short decades. Such telling changes will affect people in all sorts of ways. However, the simple nutritional explanation may not be the correct interpretation in the circumstances, as further examination of James Flynn's research suggests.

The reason why Flynn argues that the Japanese IQ gains have in fact been substantially greater than Lynn originally suggested is that the baseline – namely American scores – had itself changed. Americans, too, had put on something in the order of seven IQ points. According to Professor Neil McKintosh of Cambridge University:

We have very little idea of what environmental changes could be sufficient to produce this sort of change in IQ in North America over the last 25 years. The only changes one can imagine that have reasonably occurred in North America from the early 1950s to the mid-1970s are some economic changes. Undoubtedly there's been some improvement in the economic circumstance of average North Americans. There has presumably been some improvement in education, although we're talking about the IQ scores of young children rather than of adolescents or adults. So if we're going to appeal to education to explain these changes we have to appeal to very early education, indeed even perhaps to pre-school education.

Neil McKintosh goes further than this. He believes that no one really understands what has happened to produce these changes in IQ scores in America. He adds:

> Equally, I don't think anybody has any notion of what the changes could have been in Japan that have caused a 15-point change in IQ over a 25-year period. One can certainly appeal to some obvious large changes in Japanese society, but many IQ testers for many years now have been claiming that IQ is remarkably resistant to anything other than gross, extreme environmental effects, that normal ranges of environment have only rather small effects on IQ. I think that both Lynn's data and Flynn's re-analysis of those data suggest that IQ testers are going to have to think again about that claim. (*BBC Radio 4, 7 March 1983, 'Science Now'*)

The plot thickens . . .
The latest twist in the rising IQ tale comes from a massive analysis by James Flynn of the patterns of IQ change in no

fewer than 14 European countries every year for three decades. This time the population tested was not young school or pre-school children, but military conscripts. Again, the results are, to put it mildly, astonishing. Again, gains were recorded, but this time they were as much as 25 points in a single generation. In Holland, for example, when 18-year-old recruits were given a test called Raven's Progressive Matrices, just over 30 per cent got more than 24 out of 40 items correct in 1952. In 1982 the number getting more than 24 items right had shot up to over 80 per cent. Taken over the whole range of 14 countries it was not uncommon to find average gains within the 30-year period of 18 or 20 points.

Now one ready explanation might be that, over the years, people are simply getting better at taking IQ tests. The more one is exposed to certain types of questions, the more adept one becomes at answering them. It is a bit like doing a particular crossword. When you capture the puzzle setter's style, you are half-way to solving the riddle. However, Flynn himself does not regard this as a satisfactory explanation. 'There is,' he states, 'indirect evidence that test sophistication is not a major factor.' There comes a point where 'saturation' is reached and the sophistication effect begins to level out. Nor does Flynn espouse the view that socio-economic improvements have brought about these sharp rises in scores. Certainly not to the extent he has uncovered. He concedes that better living standards might contribute up to 5 or 6 points of observed improvement. But for the other 15 points or more we have to look elsewhere. A leading British researcher, Dr Chris Brand, sums it up thus: '*Perhaps* higher IQ people have mated more assortatively (i.e., with others of "their own kind") over this period; there has been more outbreeding; family sizes are smaller; there's less lead plumbing. Any of those factors might be invoked to account for some fraction of the gain, but whether there is some big factor, yielding generational changes, is the matter of interest.'

It looks very much to James Flynn as if there is some big, as yet unidentified environmental factor behind his findings, some mysterious 'Factor X' embedded within an environment with which we are wholly familiar. In a paper titled 'Massive IQ Gains in 14 Nations: What IQ Tests Really Measure' he asks fellow psychologists to look hard for forces operating in society to improve IQ scores that could easily be overlooked because they are so commonplace.

> The fact that the factors are unknown does not mean that when identified, they will prove exotic or unfamiliar. Television and greater exposure to information stimuli of all sorts join formal schooling as possibilities. Nonetheless the factors at work must be identified, and their great potency poses the real problem. When Archimedes wanted to impress Hiero with the power of the lever, he took a ship in dry dock, heavy laden with many passengers and freight, and clasping the end of a compound pulley, drew her along smoothly as if moving under full sail at sea. It would be uninformative to say that Archimedes was using something familiar, his muscles, because without his knowledge of the principle of the lever, what he could do with his muscles was quite inexplicable.

From this analogy, Flynn goes on to make his appeal to us not to miss the wood for the trees: 'If environmental factors have an unanticipated potency, at least in advanced societies like the Netherlands, it does no good to stress their familiarity. We must look at the environment with new eyes and try to identify the unknown forces that have done so much to transform the factors we know.'

Flynn's researches, then, leave us with the riddle of some

familiar but unspecified Factor X in the environment that shapes IQ scores. However, they also leave us with another intriguing thought: that 'IQ tests do not measure intelligence'.

IQ differences are not intelligence differences

One might reasonably expect a high IQ to be reflected in a high level of educational attainment. Indeed, as we saw in Chapter 1, the notion that an IQ test is a way of identifying those with superior potential for academic achievement has long been a cornerstone of the whole rationale for testing. Oddly enough, this does not seem to hold true for the 14-nation study.

Consider, for example, these observations made by James Flynn. In the Netherlands alone the IQ scores have risen so markedly that there should be over 30,000 people who qualify as potential geniuses – with IQs over 150. 'The result,' argues Flynn, 'should be a cultural renaissance too great to be overlooked.' However, when a French research bureau surveyed the actual state of affairs in Holland, there was apparently no evidence of a dramatic increase in 'genius' as reflected in mathematical and scientific discovery among the present generation. No one points to the current crop of Dutch schoolchildren as visibly superior in intellectual talents to earlier cohorts. Where the Dutch have clearly improved, it seems, is not in mental but physical accomplishment: they are superb athletes. On the other hand, the number of inventions as recorded in the Dutch patents office has actually declined: in the 1980s the number of patents fell to only two-thirds of what it was in the 1960s.

What this means is that IQ as measured by such tests as the well-known Raven's Progressive Matrices Test does not directly measure 'intelligence' as such, but is correlated with it in a rather weak causal relationship. Just as an aerial photograph of a city, says Flynn, gives a pretty good idea of its population, so too does an IQ test score relate to intelligence. But if a city's total area doubles in, say, 30 years, this does not mean that its population has also doubled. Other factors can intervene, such as inner city decay, the spread of affluent but sparsely populated suburbs and an increase in private cars. All these can make a city bigger without the population rate being implicated at all.

What is true of the Raven's Matrices Test may also be true of other well-known IQ instruments. Until now there do not seem to be enough data on which to form a definite judgement, so Flynn concludes that, until these data *are* available, 'psychologists should stop saying that IQ tests measure intelligence'. They should also presumably not regard any differences in IQ score improvements over time, such as between the French and the English, or the Germans and the Dutch, as unequivocal differences in 'intelligence' improvements. If tests do not properly measure intelligence, then comparisons of intelligence based on such tests become, automatically, invalid.

Better deliveries

Before we leave the issue of comparative IQ improvements among nations, there is one phenomenon that could well explain upward trends. It is pointed to by J. J. Ray in a letter to *The Psychologist*, and concerns changes in obstetric practice. Nowadays surgical intervention in the case of a difficult delivery is pretty well routine in the developed world. If problems arise, doctors move in and perform an episiotomy or caesarian section. But it was not always thus. Before World War Two such procedures were rare. Instead of an episiotomy to enlarge the opening from which the baby emerged, the midwife would practise 'holding back'. That is, the baby's head, at that age not protected by a bony skull, was used to force the enlargement of the aperture: 'A common result was that babies were born a nice shade of blue due to oxygen deficiency. The trauma to the infant brain can only be imagined.'

Thus it could be that modern obstetric practices, reducing as they do the damage to the sensitive newborn's brain, have led directly to brighter children. So the perceived improvements in IQ, argues J. J. Ray, could well reflect true differences. They are not an artefact, as Flynn and others would argue, of culturally-biased tests or other imperfections in measuring intelligence, but the direct result of children coming into the world with untraumatized brains.

Not all change is upwards

Between 1963 and 1980 the American population appeared to become markedly less intelligent. At least this was the case if one equates intelligence with performance on the well-known Scholastic Aptitude Test – the SAT – because in that period the average score dropped from 490 to 445. During his term of presidency Jimmy Carter was aware of the decline and commissioned an investigation into the likely reasons. No fewer than 79 hypotheses were advanced, ranging from drugs, parental neglect, poor teacher training, environmental pollution, too much television viewing and nuclear weapons testing.

Then, in 1980, came another surprise. The downward trend went into reverse and the SAT scores started to creep up again. The 79 hypotheses looked decidedly shaky, because none of the environmental influences put forward to explain the earlier decline had undergone any profound change. Children still watched as much if not more television; the drug pushers were still making big money outside the school gates; there had been no sudden upsurge in teacher training and so on. The 1980 rise, although heartening (especially to the incumbent of the White House, Ronald Reagan, who came to power in precisely the year that American intellectual levels took their upturn), appeared inexplicable, a freak perhaps in the long-term pattern, as the earlier decline had been. But for Professor Robert Zajonc of the University of Michigan there was no mystery and no statistical aberration. He had predicted the rise four years earlier in 1976 and he had, furthermore, stated unequivocally that it would continue for 16 to 18 years – until the late 1990s – and then another decline would set in.

Family size and birth order
Zajonc believes, in common with many other behavioural scientists, that the intellectual environment provided by the family has a significant influence on the mental development of the children. What is more, he contends in what he calls his 'confluence model' that this intellectual environment changes as new children join the family and the number of children will of necessity shape it. In sum, his argument is: 'The greater the number of children and the shorter the intervals between successive births, the less mature, on the average, is the intellectual milieu for each child.' Thus the only child, being surrounded by two adults, hears mainly adult language and absorbs a richer vocabulary than a child in a larger family. In very large families the child is likely to have the company of several younger, and therefore intellectually immature, siblings during the critical formative years.

Birth order too is important in intellectual performance. Firstborns generally score higher than later-born children on tests of intellectual performance, though if children are spaced fairly widely a second-born may have a more favourable intellectual environment than the first because he or she is surrounded by more mature individuals than the firstborn. Only children are disadvantaged in Zajonc's confluence model of intellectual development because they do not have any younger children to help. By teaching his little brother or sister how to play games, what certain words mean and so on, argues Zajonc, a child benefits intellectually himself.

By studying the birth patterns in America, Zajonc was able to predict that, with the drop in family size from 1962 onwards, SAT scores would begin to rise when the children involved reached the age when they would be tested. Similarly, with the established rise in the US birthrate after 1980, he expects the scores of children tested towards the end of the century to show a decline. 'Even if there are drastic changes in our educational system – deterioration or reform – ' says Zajonc, 'the pattern of SAT trends will follow the pattern of orders of births . . . because the factors that are responsible for a significant part of the decline and rise of SATs until 2002 have *already* exercised their effects.' However, and this is a hopeful note, the amount of rise or fall in SAT scores is not wholly determined by family size and birth order. Education can influence both to an enormous degree.

Just how true this is, and just how we can structure our education to promote intelligence, we shall explore in the next chapter.

8

FOSTERING THE
OUTWARD URGE

As every thinking teacher knows, the trouble with education is that it is too often about teaching and not enough about learning. Some children might sit dumbly in a classroom being talked at by a string of teachers, responding dully to what is on offer and never generating much enthusiasm for regurgitating the lessons for the purpose of homework or examinations. Yet outside school those same kids are transformed. On the way home he buys a new book on his latest hobby – tropical fish or computer games – or she visits the local library to look up a reference book on Portugal or athletics champions. They seem to be quite different people. When given things to learn they are unresponsive. When driven by curiosity to acquire knowledge they do so with a powerful thirst.

If only all education produced students like this: self-motivated, inquisitive; happy to be finding out. If it were so, learning would be akin to exploration. Schooldays would be like those adventurous pre-school years when the very young infant is seeing, hearing, touching and smelling the great uncharted world and trying to make sense of it. And, as he or she begins to understand it, making contact and communicating with it in an ever-enriching two-way process of discovery and stimulus. If only education as stipulated and practised by teaching establishments could capture – or rather re-capture – something of this sort of exploratory excitement.

In this book we have seen a new picture of intelligence emerge: not one thing, but many; not unique to *Homo sapiens*, but widespread throughout the animal kingdom; not a froth on the solid brew of our vital qualifications for biological survival, but the key to them.

It is clear that some of us are born with more intellectual muscle than others. It is also clear that the differences are slight, even between those we call geniuses and the rest of us. Might there then be some way to bridge the gap between them and us?

Can we increase our intelligence in some way? Or at the very least make the best of what we have got? In this chapter we will be considering some of the ways in which we might improve on nature.

Hot houses

The luxuriant growth of tropical plants in hot houses has been seen by some as a model for the way we should treat our children. Why not, runs the theory, give them the intellectual equivalent of the plant house?

In Venice during the eighteenth century, the orphanage for girls called *la Pietà* sought to encourage musical skills. It employed, among others, the composer Vivaldi to help the children. The outcome was that an unusually high number of these girls became musicians of quality. Equally, anyone who has seen a herd of child violinists trained by the Suzuki method will not doubt that it is possible to turn a child into a competent musician quite early in its life. There are many anecdotes from history of the child prodigy, nurtured by his parents or some other well-meaning adult, achieving exceptional mental accomplishments. Perhaps the most famous of psychologists, William James, was brought up in a family that travelled widely, and in which the children were encouraged to extract every last morsel from their experiences, and to write about them. The James family was independently wealthy, but no matter. There is a lesson there for all.

Better babies for all

One example of the extraordinary results that can be achieved is the case of Ruth Lawrence.

Ruth Lawrence is the product of an extraordinary drive by her father, Harry Lawrence. He is a one-time teacher turned computer consultant, who was determined that his daughter should have the best possible education. And the best possible person to educate her was himself. From the outset, he and his wife Sylvia encouraged Ruth to explore the limits of her curiosity. They believed that the child's natural interest in the world around her could be harnessed to teach her more efficiently than if she were taught within the regimented confines of a school. The result was that at the age of five Ruth had the reading ability of a nine-year-old, and had started to learn mathematics. Harry Lawrence gave up his job to concentrate on teaching her. He used a form of Socratic dialogue – questions and answers were used to guide the child to learn. At nine Ruth passed O-level mathematics. At ten she came top in the entrance examination for St Hugh's College, Oxford. At eleven she passed five A-levels, at thirteen she was awarded first-class honours in mathematics. To obtain her degree, she answered 81 questions over 10 papers: the average student manages about 30. She completed her course in two years instead of the normal three, and went on to study for a doctorate.

So, a genius? Harry Lawrence denies that his daughter is more than averagely special. He puts her achievement down to hard work. Ruth studies for eight hours a day, and works very quickly. She has also had the advantage of a well-informed and extremely committed teacher. Some have argued that bringing up children in this way can compromise their emotional development. They fear that Ruth will end up unable to make relationships with others. The fears appear unfounded. A further question remains. Ruth is one of a very select group and, despite her father's assertion that most of her accomplishment is due to application, it is by no means obvious that any child placed in the same circumstances would end up in the same way.

The best known of recent attempts at hot-housing groups of children is Glenn Doman's Institute for the Achievement of Human Potential in Philadelphia.

Doman believes that every child contains the seeds of genius. Put them in the right soil, apply appropriate fertilizer, raise to the right temperature – and there you are, a prize-winning product. His technique is to present children with almost continuous stimulation of some sort. Bright lights are shone into the eyes of infants. Loud noises are sounded behind their heads. Parents talk to them, give them puzzles, encourage every activity imaginable from the mental to the physical. The results appear to be quite spectacular: children of four and five conversing in Japanese, extensive mathematical abilities, in algebra for instance, musical talent to make Dr Suzuki look in his violin case again.

Too young to learn?
Those opposed to hot-housing frequently argue that young children are simply incapable of absorbing complex ideas and concepts. The Yale University psychologist Dr Robert Sternberg finds this idea unacceptable:

> We have this phoney idea that young kids can't understand higher processes, that they don't think in complex ways. And the reason I say it's a phoney idea is any parent should know better. They'll have kids who are two, three, who are manipulating them into buying toys. Or manipulating them into getting their way in terms of bedtime and so on. On the one hand they're saying that the kid isn't very smart, and doesn't understand things. On the other hand, the parent is being manipulated. I mean you're manipulated from when the kid's born and starts crying. I remember as a kid feeling exactly the way my kid's feeling now. I was thinking what suckers adults were, that they didn't realize how much we understood about what was going on, and it was often to our advantage that they didn't

understand. It's sort of like the successful salesman is not the person who comes off as the high pressure salesman. So we were glad they didn't know too much. But kids can do a lot more than we give them credit for.

At Cambridge University, Dr Judy Dunn has found other evidence to support Sternberg's view. She and her colleague Carol Kendrick decided to test the psychologist's orthodoxy that children are incapable of mature understanding until they are five or so. They studied the social interactions that go on between brothers and sisters – the longest relationship anyone is likely to have. What emerged from an extensive study of a number of families was quite startling. It appears that children as young as 14 or 15 months can show a sophisticated understanding of the moods and intentions of another child. So in a family with a new-born second child, the older would frequently comment on the baby's behaviour and make predictions about what it would do. Another, and perhaps less attractive, feature of the children's behaviour was that they lived up to the description 'little horrors'. They seemed to know how best to tease their siblings. They knew how to provoke, irritate, and manipulate them. The older child also seemed prone to taking away the younger one's favourite object in moments of temper.

The significance of Dr Dunn's findings is that they show that very young children can grasp complicated matters, even without formal schooling. If she is right, there seems to be no intellectual reason why hot-housing should not work.

Like most other theories concerning intelligence, hot-housing has its opponents. It is too early at the moment to see whether children hot-housed by Doman's methods grow up to sustain their accelerated early learning, and whether the experience has any detrimental effect on their personalities. An impressive array of child psychologists, educationalists, doctors, and scientists see very little but bad in Doman's work. They believe that any gains will be short-lived, and that the potential for severe psychiatric disturbance in children placed under so much pressure must result in a lot of unhappy adults. The jury, however, is still out. What appears to be certain is, if you want your child to speak Japanese, start now.

Baby tests

A very young baby sits comfortably in a reclining chair. In front of her is a screen. Out of sight is an experimenter who projects on to the screen a pair of photographs, both of faces. One of the faces the child has seen before, the other is totally novel. Using a television monitor, the researcher carefully measures the amount of time the baby spends looking at each face. The data are recorded and logged with similar timings taken from other children less than six months old. The experiment measures visual attentiveness. But it also reveals an interesting link with the performance of the children on standard IQ tests when they reach school age. Babies that spend comparatively less time looking at familiar photos tend to score higher on IQ tests. Why this should be so is an intriguing question that could shed light on the whole process of intelligence. Other researchers have extended the technique beyond faces to see whether babies differ in their responses to old and new patterns or abstract geometric shapes. Sure enough, again there are differences.

Dr Robert Plomin of Pennsylvania State University finds such results significant because 'the babies are telling you they recognize the difference between the old picture and the new – that's the key. They are not just discriminating between the two. They are showing you that they remember the old picture.' This capacity seems to be an important mental process in infancy for learning and thinking. It sheds light on the information-processing abilities of the child, showing how it deals with novelty, which is fundamental to intelligent behaviour.

At a very early age, then, it seems as if one could predict something about a child's intelligence simply by studying its degree of visual attentiveness, at least in part: to be precise, 25–36 per cent, for that is the percentage of variance in IQ which can be attributed to this measure of attentiveness. That still leaves a lot of room for environmental influences to act, because 64–75 per cent of the variance in IQ at the age of six cannot be accounted for by the attentiveness test. For this reason the researchers themselves warn against placing too much weight on the predictive power of such tests. And they are quick to deny that a baby's intellectual destiny is sealed at birth, simply because they have discovered a firm but wholly statistical correlation between attentiveness and IQ scores.

However, the finding may prove to be valuable. If low-birth-weight babies or other youngsters at risk for poor school performance later on could be tested routinely, it might be possible to identify those who need special care to raise academic performance.

Intelligence in context

The psychologist H. J. Butcher writes:
There is not much we can do about the genes people are born with, but there is a great deal we can do about improving social conditions and educational practice . . . Even in countries self-labelled as democratic, it is hardly possible to deny that a large proportion of the population is suffering intellectual and cultural depri-

vation in one form or another, and that very few people
are able fully to develop their potential talents.

It is equally hard to deny that the way children are brought
up and the surroundings they are brought up in do have an
effect on their abilities. And not just in the case of pressured
environments such as hot-housing. There is a great deal of
evidence from research on children living in poor housing,
or – fairly obviously – those unable to obtain good quality
education.

The effects of deprivation take root in the early years. For
instance, a study in 1964, reported in *Stability and Change
in Human Characteristics* by B. S. Bloom, showed that those
unfortunate enough to find themselves in bad surroundings
between the ages of one and four would suffer the intellectual
effects for the rest of their lives. The American obsession
with differences in intelligence between whites and blacks
provides a useful window on the effects of environment.

The irony about the history of testing for black–white
differences is that the results have not always come out in
favour of the whites. In 1897, for instance, a gentleman
called Steson found that black children were better at memo-
rizing poetry than were whites. By the early 1900s, however,
most studies appeared to show that the average IQ of black
people was in the mid-80s. What rapidly became clear,
though, was that it was almost impossible to remove or
correct for the effects of various influences on IQ outside
inherited capability. These factors included such things as
social position, motivation, language difficulties, and even
the influence of the tester. At the beginning of World War
One another anomaly was thrown up. The average IQ of
blacks from the northern states entering the army was *higher*
than that of white recruits from the south. Further research
uncovered another interesting fact. If the differences in
measured intelligence between whites and blacks were corre-

lated with the place where the studies were done, then it turned out that there was hardly any difference in New York, rather more in Chicago, and more and more as the Deep South was approached. It also appeared that the IQ of a particular black person went up the longer he or she lived in the north. More recent work has underlined the point that any observed differences in intelligence can almost certainly be accounted for by external factors.

As we have seen in Chapter 2, the issue of the heritability of intelligence and racial differences in IQ has been a political football. There are still those who claim that genes play the major role in determining intelligence. But it does now appear that no one seriously doubts that better social conditions lead to higher measured intelligence. Following his study of West Indian children in Britain in the 1960s, Peter Vernon concluded: ' . . . it is clear that the most important single factor in children's performance on g and verbal tests is the cultural level of the home, parental education and encouragement, reading facilities and probably the speech background . . . Economic level as such is subsidiary.'

It is bad enough that depriving children of the appropriate surroundings can lead to low intelligence. But perhaps more disturbing is that the process can continue as they get older. Several studies of people who live isolated lives – gypsies and mountain communities, for example – demonstrate that some sort of social life is essential to fuel the development of intelligence.

'Some sort of social life' is, of course, begging the question. A social life of sorts exists in children's institutions, yet those brought up in them usually score badly on IQ tests. In contrast, children placed in foster homes where the foster-parents are concerned to see the child get on do rather better than expected. This is another complex and convoluted story. The message is clear, though.

Happy homes and interested parents make bright children.

What then does all this mean for the education of our children? In his book *Human Intelligence*, H. J. Butcher concludes:

> Psychological views of intelligence have played some part in . . . underestimating and wastage of national resources. The idea of a fixed, unalterable IQ has led to the idea of a fixed, unalterable quantity of national talent . . . (But) whatever proportion of variance in intelligence we ascribe to hereditary or genetic endowment, for practical purposes we must act and plan as though environmental influences were crucial . . . There is a strong likelihood that the genes set a limit or ceiling on cognitive ability, but that in most people's lives environmental circumstances impose a much lower one . . . Social organization . . . is capable of such a degree of change and development that 'what is given at birth' may, in different forms of society, assume almost any degree of relative importance.

In other words, let us not worry too much about what people are born with, let us find ways of enabling them to make the best of it. This view finds support from Howard Gardner.

Educating many minds

> The design of my ideal school of the future is based upon two assumptions. The first is that not all people have the same interests and abilities: not all of us learn in the same way. The second assumption is the one that hurts: it is the assumption that nowadays no one person can learn everything there is to learn . . . Choice is inevitable . . . the choices we make for

ourselves, and for the people who are under our charge, might as well be informed choices.

As we have seen, Howard Gardner believes that there are certain types of intelligence. In Chapter 2 we identified seven: there may be more. Gardner also believes that every one of us is born with what he calls 'certain core abilities in each of the Intelligences'. But after birth, he thinks that each of us follows a 'trajectory' as our abilities develop. So in the first year of life we acquire 'raw patterning ability', which shows itself as discrimination of musical notes, or appreciation of what a three-dimensional structure means. The child showing promise in a particular Intelligence will show most ability to establish and perceive patterns in that area.

The next stage is the use of symbols. So sentences, songs, drawings, gestures, all show that the child has begun to appreciate the value of symbols in each particular Intelligence.

Next comes a 'notational system'. This allows the child to write down, or make some sort of record, of what he or she has been expressing through the previous use of symbols. Then, during adolescence and the years immediately after, the Intelligences begin to manifest themselves in vocational ability. So the child who was able early to manipulate patterns and the symbols and notation of mathematics, starts to show promise as a mathematician, or in an occupation demanding mathematical skills.

Gardner's observations extend to what we might call geniuses – people exceptionally well-talented in a particular Intelligence. As he points out: 'It is not important that *all* members of the Puluwat tribe demonstrate precocious spatial abilities needed for navigation by the stars, nor is it necessary for all Westerners to master mathematics to the degree necessary to make a significant contribution to theoretical physics. So long as the individuals "at promise" in particular domains are located efficiently, the overall knowledge of the group will be advanced in all domains.'

Another consequence of Howard Gardner's multiple intelligence theory is that it is very important that the right sort of education be available at the right time. Different sensitivity to instruction at different times during the child's development makes it vital that attempts to educate in notational systems, for example, are not given too early. The child will simply get nothing from them. In addition, adolescent children are seen to need career counselling from someone who can assess the relative strengths of the Intelligences within them. And here is the core of Gardner's proposals – better assessment.

Unsurprisingly, Gardner is not happy with conventional pencil-and-paper tests of intelligence. For him, they are locked rigidly into the domain of only one of the Intelligences. Children who score badly on these sorts of tests might have very high promise in activities demanding the exercise of another Intelligence. Gardner therefore proposes that schools should have what he calls 'assessment specialists', charged with trying to understand the broad sweep of abilities of each child under their care. Clearly, it is necessary to develop tests that can measure directly prowess in a particular Intelligence before the assessment specialists can get on with their work. It is no good, for example, trying to assess musical intelligence by purely verbal methods. One way in which this might be done is being investigated in 'Project Spectrum'.

Here, Gardner and his colleagues equip a school with a wide variety of materials designed to encourage play across the range of the pupil's Intelligences. The child is not directed towards any specific activity. Rather, it is allowed to make its own choices about which things are most attractive, which offer most opportunities for fun. The teacher monitors closely how long the child spends exerting the powers of each Intelligence, and the kinds of things it does during play. The result is a 'spectrum profile', a description of a child's strengths and weaknesses in each cognitive area. The profile also makes suggestions for ways to nurture and augment the child's talents.

There is a caution for teachers within Gardner's theory. He points out that one of the reasons why some children have difficulty in some subjects might be that the medium for instruction cannot carry the message sufficiently strongly. Take a child who is weak in mathematical intelligence. Even though he or she might be strong at linguistic skills, attempts to explain mathematics through words will flounder. There is no direct way to translate the language of mathematics, which is difficult for the child, into the easier-to-comprehend language of English. It is then up to the teacher to try to find an instructional route through some other medium. Perhaps it is not too fanciful to think of teaching mathematics through dance. Anyway, the upshot is that teachers must try harder.

Gardner weaves a convincing argument with a ringing conclusion. But he himself points out caveats:

> While Multiple Intelligence Theory is consistent with much empirical evidence, it has not been subjected to strong experimental tests within psychology. Within the area of education, the applications of the theory are even more tentative and speculative. Our hunches will have to be revised many times in light of actual classroom experience. Still there are important reasons for considering the theory of Multiple Intelligences and its implications for education. First of all, it is clear that many talents, if not Intelligences, are overlooked nowadays; individuals with these talents are the chief casualties of the single-minded, single-funnelled approach to the mind. There are many unfilled or poorly

filled niches in our society and it would be opportune
to guide individuals with the right set of abilities to
these billets. Finally, our world is beset with problems;
to have any chance of solving them, we must make the
very best use of the Intelligences we possess. Perhaps
recognizing the plurality of Intelligences and the mani-
fold ways in which human individuals may exhibit
them is an important first step.

Howard Gardner is already trying out his ideas practically.
He is working with the staff of the Key School in Indian-
apolis. The school has been trying to develop the range of
Intelligences in its students as one of its explicit goals.
Extensive use is made of projects; there is a different one
four times a year, each lasting about 8 or 9 weeks. The
themes are very broad, indeed almost nebulous: harmony,
or patterns, would be examples. Every student in the school
has to create something which exemplifies the theme. The
projects are put on display, so that everyone in the school
can then see what the others have been up to. Then each
child presents his or her project to his or her class. They
describe the background and how they came up with their
concept. There is then a sort of project press conference, in
which questions are posed and answers given. This is recorded on video tape. At the end of the year every child has
four projects in his or her video portfolio, plus an interview
with a video specialist about how the child is doing. By the
end of the child's time in school there are twenty or thirty
different projects recorded for all time.

So far so good, but what does Gardner do with all this
tape?

We are beginning a project of figuring how to assess
those portfolios. How to actually come up with a
description of four things. One, how does the child

conceive the project? Two, how does he or she present it? Three, what is the actual quality of the project, which is important too? And four, what kind of individualizing features of this human being come through on the project? I think we can do this. I think we can provide this information on the report card, just the way we give information on spelling. I think this information could be tremendously important for next year's teacher, for the parents, and most important, for the student himself or herself because the student gets a kind of evolving map of how his or her abilities of conceiving and understanding and presenting evolve over the years.

I think we're going to be able to do this in a relatively reliable and objective way, and I think it gives an entirely new dimension to assessment. And a dimension which is much more important once you get out of school. It's really ironic. We take hundreds, if not thousands of tests in school over the fifteen years we're in school. Once we leave school we almost never take a test again. What we're being given all the time are projects to carry out to the satisfaction of other people and ourselves. There's very little experience in school in carrying out projects, and virtually none in assessing them. So that's what I'm trying to push for.

Some people have attempted to damn Gardner with faint praise. They point out that all he is saying is common sense. The criticism does not worry Gardner.

I don't think there's anything wrong with saying what's common sense. What's interesting is sometimes how the science diverges so far from common sense. What I think I've done is to provide a set of labels and categories which, if you will, systematize common sense a bit. So instead of talking about people having many talents and combinations of talents, we can talk about what those talents are. And I have no objection to using the word talent, provided that we're willing to call language a talent, and logic a talent, too. I think the mistake we make is to put language and logic on a pedestal as if they're different from spatial abilities or understanding other people, and I just don't think they are.

A miracle in Milwaukee

Find a group of black mothers who score below 75 in the conventional IQ test. Take their children and give them something rather special in the way of education. From soon after birth to the beginning of ordinary schooling, subject them to seven hours a day, five days a week of intensive training. See what happens.

This experiment was actually performed in Milwaukee. What happened was that the children exhibited an apparently astonishing gain in IQ. Compared to another group of children at one year old, the IQs were about the same. But by the time they were three, the average IQ of the experimental group was over 120, some 30 points higher than the average for the control group. There was some narrowing in this gap over the years, and some adjustments to take account of changing testing methods. Nevertheless, the experimental children entered adolescence 10 points ahead.

This seems like very good support for hot-housing. Early intensive education can improve a child's abilities significantly. Unfortunately for avid gardeners, the study has some problems. Chief of these is that the scientists who conducted it have seemed remarkably reticent about publishing their findings. In 1972 they promised a final report. It was never published, presumably because the project's director was spending time keeping himself out of the clutches of government investigators. He was, in fact, eventually convicted for the misuse of official funds. Small wonder that little faith has been placed in the project's findings.

One group of scientists did decide, though, to see if they could produce their own miracle. The Abecedarian Project at the University of North Carolina used broadly similar children and techniques. It too found some increase in measured IQ early in life, but by the time the children had entered ordinary schools, the difference was, at best, marginal.

Triarchic education

We have this illusion that the smart person has to be good at everything. I don't think it's true. If you look at people who are really smart in their everyday lives, what you find is that they're usually good at something, but it may be just one thing, or it may be two things, and that's it. The people who are practically smart are people who know what they're good at. They know what they're not good at. And they capitalize on or make the most of their strengths and they find ways around their weaknesses, they find ways of compensating.

Robert Sternberg's triarchic theory of intelligence (Chapter 2) places the emphasis not on academic, intellectual achievement, but on how well an individual can get on in the outside world. Say you are invited to visit someone in a strange city. You have the address and a map. The house is only five minutes' walk from your hotel, but you are very bad at map reading. It takes you an hour to get there. Now what is the intelligent, the smart thing, to do? Spend hours learning orienteering, trying to massage into life a skill you might not even possess? No, says Robert Sternberg. Get someone else to drive you. By shifting your needs away from your inadequacies, you can give every appearance of being highly intelligent in a field in which you are really no more than, or even below, average.

Are these things we can learn in school? At the moment, the answer appears to be 'no'. Sternberg has been studying managers in business. He gives them what he calls a 'tacit knowledge' test. That is, he tests them against a list of things acknowledged to be essential to the successful businessman. These turn out to be the things that you are not taught explicitly, either in school or even on the job. It is the knowledge you gain just by doing something. As Sternberg points out, it is very different being in a job to being in preparation for that job.

So can these intelligence-enhancing skills be developed? Sternberg certainly thinks so. Like Gardner, he is developing his own version of the intelligence test. It will aim to evaluate intelligence across a very broad range. The idea is not to get a number, but to arrive at some sort of profile of strengths and weaknesses. Training can then be aimed at helping to develop the strengths and combat the weaknesses.

The test has two parts, A and B. The A form has some similarities to a conventional IQ test, but also some significant differences. It does not, for instance, have a test of vocabulary. Sternberg's view is that vocabulary is too influenced by background to make any real contribution to measuring intelligence. 'You don't bother to test the vocabulary of boys at Eton,' he says. What he includes instead is a test of a child's ability to work out the meanings of the words from their context. You have to learn the vocabulary during the course of the test. That way, prior knowledge does not become confused with intelligence. The test has scores for verbal skills, mathematical skills, and abstract reasoning skills. Unlike a conventional IQ test, these are not combined into one number: they stand on their own. The idea is that this is a fairer representation of individual abilities in each area. It also reflects the fact that people can differ radically from one domain to the next.

Another difference is that there is a test of ability to deal with novelty. Imagine you were suddenly swept up and deposited in Morocco. How well could you cope with the language, the weather, the people, and so on? The Sternberg test aims to assess this quality. Interestingly, it appears that those who are good at analytical, rational thinking, do not do so well when confronted with novel circumstances. For the purposes of his test, Sternberg will present his subjects with novelty in the form of an untrue, even absurd statement such as 'sparrows play hopscotch'. What, he asks, are the consequences of game-playing birds? Only the flexible mind comes up with some answers through a 'willing suspension of disbelief'. The test, then, requires you to imagine that something is true which happens not to be true – a measure of your ability to put yourself into a different frame of mind – that is, to deal with novelty. Dogmatic, rigid thinkers need not apply.

The third part of the test is for practical intelligence. Take two boys, John and Tom. They are discussing two baseball teams, the reds and the blues. John comments to Tom that every member of the red team is better than every member of the blue team. Can he conclude that the reds are therefore the better team? Rational analysis would suggest that they have to be. But practical experience suggests the opposite. A team with magnificent players for every position may be awful because they cannot play together. This part of the test exposes the fallacy that the whole is equal to the sum of the parts. Or to test practical figurative reasoning, the test might provide a route map for, say, the underground, and ask people to plan a route.

Once Dr Sternberg has a profile of the people he has tested, he has several strategies for helping them to enhance their intelligence.

One thing he does is to show his students what he means by an 'inferential fallacy'. He shows them how working from a set of true premises can lead to a false conclusion. Then he will give them a list of examples, some of which are fallacious, some of which are true, and ask them to sort the true from the false. He will then ask the students to try to come up with examples from their own lives of how these inferential fallacies are committed: 'It's very important for the learner to take an active role because virtually every one of those fallacies is something everyone's done, and the thing is to recognize it when you do it yourself, or when you see it in other people.'

Sternberg has his own favourite examples. One is the problem mentioned earlier of welding a group of great baseball players into a coherent team. Another is the strange phenomenon of the unrepeatable rookie. It appears that the player voted to have had the best first year in the baseball league almost always has a terrible second year. Why should this be? Perhaps the award has gone to the player's head, and he has become overconfident. Or maybe the people handing out the prize are not very good at it. These are the sorts of ordinary reasons most people come up with. But the real reason is that the players are prey to a statistical principle called regression, which also explains why the second time you go to a restaurant you really enjoyed, the meal is never as good as it was the first time.

Sternberg also places great store on the role of insight. He points out that the ability to think intuitively is a great help in solving problems. Again, his teaching strategy is to use examples.

One is the case of the high-level automobile executive. This man loves everything about his job except for one thing. He cannnot stand his boss. His problems become so bad that he decides to leave. He goes to an executive headhunter. The headhunter can certainly get him another job, but not such an enjoyable one. So what does the executive do? Bite the bullet and go off somewhere else? No. He gains insight that allows him to redefine the problem. Why not, he thinks, give his *boss's* name to the headhunter? Sure enough, the boss is offered a new job, and the now happy executive stays where he is. In fact, he is even promoted into his boss's old job.

Another example comes closer to home: from Sternberg's back yard, in fact. Like many other Americans, the Sternbergs have trouble with racoons. They knock over the rubbish bins in search of food, and strew the contents all over the ground. But, also like many other Americans, the Sternbergs are humane. They tried to catch the racoons and set them free elsewhere unharmed. But racoons are pretty good at avoiding traps, and nothing Sternberg could do would stop them. The solution? Redefine the problem. Sternberg bought rubbish bins with sealed lids . . .

The next step in the process of education is to get students to see ways to redefine problems in their own life. Often they will find better solutions to things that have been bothering them. They will have enhanced their practical intelligence. The key was in relating the thinking processes involved to the practicalities of the person's life.

This particular insight of Sternberg's leads him to make fairly harsh criticisms of the educational system. His view is that schools do not do enough to make their lessons seem relevant to the real world inhabited by the students. Teachers believe that they are paid to teach. In fact, argues Sternberg, they should be there to help students to learn. And it is difficult, if not impossible, to learn anything unless its relevance and usefulness can be seen.

It would be surprising if two such like-minded people as Robert Sternberg and Howard Gardner were not to collaborate. Currently they are attempting to find ways in which what we might call 'practical intelligence' can be taught in schools. The elements of the course are certainly practical. Missing out on them, says Sternberg, can also have dramatic effects on school performance:

> . . . a lot of kids never learn this stuff. They never learn how to study for a test, they never learn how to budget time on doing their homework. I've had this discussion with my own son Seth, what does a teacher expect when you write a paper? And we've disagreed, and if a student doesn't know what the teacher's expectations are, the student keeps not doing as well as he or she should do. So I think it's important – and I do it with my own students, I mean you know, like I'm training them, say, to become psychologists, but I don't just teach them a bunch of facts, I'll work with them on how to write a grant proposal because if you don't get grant money you're sort of out of a job real fast. And that's not what you're hired for. No one ever teaches you to do it, but you need to learn how to write a grant. It's things like, how do you manage yourself? How do you manage others? And how do you manage your tasks? How do you study? How do you allocate your time? How do you figure out what a teacher expects out of you? It would be that ilk of thing. How do you relate to the teacher in a way so that the teacher doesn't become antagonistic? If you do things and make a teacher antagonistic often it doesn't matter how smart you are, the teacher looks for a way to shove the knife

in. So it would be that ilk of thing, and it's a whole programme.

Sternberg and Gardner are proposing a radical change in the way we educate ourselves and our children. They are meeting some opposition from the educational establishment, but also, says Sternberg, a surprising amount of interest and enthusiasm.

Training for vocations

The multi-faceted view of intelligence has clear implications for career choice. Suppose, for instance, that two people apply for a vacancy as an air traffic controller. They both have the same numerical score on a test of spatial ability, but the processes they use to solve the problems are entirely different. One solves it purely visually. The other converts the problem to a verbal form, and solves it using language skills. Which would be better for the job?

Robert Sternberg has no doubts: ' . . . the person looking at the number isn't going to know that one of us did the problem spatially, and the other verbally, but do you really want to hire as an air traffic controller at Gatwick airport somebody who does the problems verbally, who's sort of talking it over to himself as two blips are coming toward each other? No.'

'Instrumental enrichment'
In the 1950s an Israeli educationalist, Reuven Feuerstein, was charged with the task of assessing the intellectual abilities of young Jewish immigrants arriving in their thousands in Israel. He had at his disposal the usual battery of IQ tests, but very soon decided that they were not at all suitable because they measured achievement and not potential: what a child had already learned, not what it might be capable

of learning. Not only that, thought Feuerstein, the whole concept of putting ranking numbers on individuals seems to be something of a self-limiting exercise. If a person believes that he or she has been 'scientifically' graded as a level 2 or 3 or 4 or whatever, that is how he or she tends to behave. Initially, then, Feuerstein began to devise new ways of testing the newcomers to the emergent Israeli state. Later he changed direction and became more concerned with teaching methods designed to get the best out of people. The result is a network of projects around the world based on a method dubbed by Feuerstein 'Instrumental Enrichment'.

In Britain his work is represented by the Oxfordshire Skills Programme. When Michael Delahaye studied the work going on in various classrooms in Oxfordshire he wrote this account of how Instrumental Enrichment works:

In a sentence, it makes children think about thinking. By intense, quasi-Talmudic sessions of question and answer, they are made aware of the discrete stages that are essential for the evaluation of experience – perception, analysis, comparison, classification, hypothesis, synthesis – all those complicated mental processes that most of us acquire naturally but which many children, often those later categorized as 'low achievers', miss out on.

In practice Feuerstein's techniques seem to work because they give 'hands-on' or rather 'brains-on' contact with many problems with which a child is confronted. Students are made to think about putting together a solution by a variety of intellectual strategies, choosing the one which works best. This puts considerable demands on their teachers, who are encouraged to be liberal with the use of such 'highbrow' terminology as 'stratagem', 'hypothesis' and 'parameter' when working with a class. They also, more fundamentally, have to rid themselves of the conventional idea that children automatically absorb information. They do not, unless they are highly motivated to do so and unless they are given the self-esteem and self-confidence that many naturally lack.

These qualities are all reflected in the achievements of the children. They seem to be more articulate and more confident than they were before, able to debate among themselves quite advanced intellectual problems in language that is undeniably more mature than most other groups of their age. When Dr Michael Shayer, a psychologist from King's College London, studied the results of Feuerstein's techniques in detail he concluded that the children had in one respect become more 'intelligent'. They were more able to process fresh experience and to integrate this into their thinking. They had definitely acquired a superior thinking skill.

However, there was no evidence that this had carried over into their other school subjects: they had not automatically become better geographers or French speakers. On the face of it then, it might seem as if Instrumental Enrichment is little more than an exercise in mental gymnastics with no relevance to real world problems. Shayer, however, turns this round the other way and asks whether the rest of the curriculum might not be out of phase with the Skills Programme:

The atmosphere of the special lessons is so markedly different from the atmosphere of the rest of their school subject lessons that they're not really tapping the same kind of learning behaviour in the pupils at all. I'm sure the pupils will have learnt all sorts of useful cognitive skills in the programme, but if they go to their maths or history lesson and they're not called upon to exercise

those skills, then it's not reasonable to expect that it
will have very much effect on their learning.

Several key points emerge from the Oxfordshire experiment.
First, that intelligence is not immutably fixed, but can be
improved by the right sort of teaching. Second, that such
teaching has to be imaginative and inspirational, rather than
coldly factual. And, third, that educational systems may
need to be more flexible to allow for somewhat unconven-
tional, even off-beat approaches to teaching within the
curriculum. All three points are interrelated and we should
keep them all in mind when meeting the challenge of
'improving intelligence levels'. Otherwise it is likely that
intelligence – that prime resource of any nation – will be
underestimated and to a large degree wasted. As we have
seen repeatedly – and Feuerstein's experiences in the 1950s
were further confirmation – it is a mistake to believe that
intelligence only means what is measured on a standard IQ
test.

Educating the society of mind

Marvin Minsky has collaborated for many years with another
mathematician-turned-psychologist, Seymour Papert. Papert worked for some time with the celebrated Swiss child
psychologist Jean Piaget, and his ideas were profoundly
influenced by Piaget's investigations of child development.

Piaget was convinced that children acquire knowledge
and abilities in stages, much as physical growth also goes
through discrete steps. Minsky and Papert developed a theory
in which the key element of this process of mental growth
was the introduction of levels of management. That is, at
each stage the child has certain resources, but whenever a
new ability, or skill, or body of knowledge is added something
has to decide which resource should be used to tackle which

problem. Hence the need for a managerial structure. Much as the company without a strong manager will quickly go to the wall, so innumerable mental skills cannot be brought to bear on a problem unless something knows they are there to be used.

Papert and Minsky, then, see childhood as a succession of building one layer after another. The lower layers have the fine details of the skills. The higher layers have knowledge about which skills should be engaged for which goals, how to resolve conflicts between them and combine two different abilities. This scheme seems plausible enough. But Minsky sees a problem:

> Now the mystery is, what impels a child to progress from one stage to another? Why doesn't it just stop and be satisfied with a certain performance? Well, there isn't any child in this theory, of course, the child is the whole organization, and there doesn't need to be a single focus that's making these long-range decisions. So one possibility is that there are genetically determined clocks which cause the nervous system to change how it learns from year to year. No one has any evidence for that sort of thing, and I think the next generation or two of brain sciences are going to reveal all sorts of thrilling discoveries about how parts of the nervous system change how they work from year to year, but right now it's a closed mystery for us.

One implication of Minsky's ideas is that, until we have a better knowledge of these biological mechanisms underlying development, it will be impossible for us to manipulate our teaching to take advantage of them. We do not know, for instance, which of our learning patterns are imposed upon us by the nature of the ideas we are trying to learn, and which by our biological abilities and shortcomings.

Minsky has no doubts about what we should teach in the interim, though – thinking skills. His view is that every teacher and every educator knows that teaching people to think is a very good idea. The snag is that we have no idea how to go about it, mainly because we do not know how thinking works. He is not downcast by this, however:

> I'm very optimistic about this in the sense that when one or another of these theories of how the mind works, and by mind, I just mean how the brain works, when we get a really adequate theory, then it'll be clear how you can intervene in education to improve the situation. It's just that the different theories are so incomparable and chaotic and inadequate that almost all teachers know in their hearts that it doesn't pay to try to teach children a new theory of psychology.

Even so, the psychological insights that Seymour Papert gained may be useful to us now. It might seem a good idea to bolster children's confidence by telling them that they are unique, that there is something special about the ability to think. Papert had the opposite insight. He observed that telling children that they are only thinking machines could be extremely liberating for them, could enable them to overcome thinking obstacles. Take, for example, the child who is bad at mathematics. Folklore has it that some people are good at maths, others bad, and there is nothing you can do about it. What usually happens to the child who is bad at maths is that it will say to itself: 'Ah, I'm no good at this. Let me find something else to do.' The child has decided that the fault is within itself, that there is some defect of intelligence or character that prevents it being good at maths. It will then never learn. What Papert does is to get the child to think about itself as a package of little processors. If the problem lies with arithmetic, for instance, then Papert's strategy is to get the child to say: 'It's not me that's having trouble, it's just one little piece of machinery that's not up to this job.' This leads it to think that perhaps there is a solution. It is not a general inability to do maths, it is just a small failure of a small component of the whole spectrum of intelligence. And, most importantly, it can probably be fixed, or another little machine can be used instead. Once the child accepts this, learning becomes a constructive, intellectual challenge rather than a question of social inadequacy. A technical hitch, not a moral taint.

Giving children self-confidence and the ability to overcome obstacles is obviously useful in their education. Minsky would go further, though, and suggest a similar attitude for adults. There is another piece of folklore which says that learning becomes more and more difficult as we get older. Its proponents point out how difficult it is for adults to learn foreign languages, whereas children just pick them up. But Minsky points out that children take seven or eight years to acquire linguistic competence. In the right circumstances an adult can learn more in less time than a child – witness language cramming courses for businessmen and diplomats. The main problem is motivation. By the time we reach adulthood, we have acquired enough skills to get by in the world. Why then spend precious time learning new ones? Surely it is better to take a skill at which one is already proficient and hone it, than to start from scratch in some unexplored field? But that should not stop us from trying. Most of us will know someone who is always learning new skills, or studying new fields. There is no reason why everyone cannot do the same. If you sincerely want to be smart, it is never too late to learn.

BIBLIOGRAPHY

Blakemore, Colin, *Mechanics of the Mind*, Cambridge University Press 1977

Blakemore, Colin, and Greenberg, Susan (eds), *Mindwaves*, Blackwell 1987

Block, Ned, and Dworkin, Gerald (eds), *The IQ Controversy*, Quartet Books 1977

Bloom, B. S., *Stability and Change in Human Characteristics*, Wiley 1964

Butcher, H. J., *Human Intelligence – Its Nature and Assessment*, Methuen & Co. 1970

CIBA Foundation Symposium 69 (new series), *Brain and Mind*, Excerpta Medica 1979

Colinvaux, Paul, *Why Big Fierce Animals Are Rare*, George Allen and Unwin 1980

Evans, Christopher, *Landscapes of the Night*, Gollancz 1983

Evans, Peter, *Ourselves and other Animals*, Century 1987

Evans, Peter, and Deehan, Geoff, *The Keys to Creativity*, Grafton 1988

Feigenbaum, Edward, and McCorduch, Pamela, *The Fifth Generation*, Michael Joseph 1983

Gardner, Howard, *Frames of Mind*, Paladin 1985

Gazzaniga, Michael, *The Social Brain*, Basic Books 1985

Gilling, Dick, and Brightwell, Robin, *The Human Brain*, Orbis 1982

Gould, Stephen Jay, *The Mismeasure of Man*, W. W. Norton & Company Inc. 1981

Gregory, Richard (ed), *The Oxford Companion to the Mind*, Oxford University Press 1987

Griffin, D. R., *Animal Thinking*, Harvard University Press 1984

Humphrey, Nicholas, *The Inner Eye*, Channel 4/Faber & Faber 1986

Hunt, Morton, *The Universe Within*, The Harvester Press 1982

Kamin, Leon, *The Science and Politics of IQ*, Penguin 1977

Minsky, Marvin, *The Society of Mind*, Heinemann 1987

Moravec, Hans, *Mind Children: The Future of Robot and Human Intelligence*, Harvard University Press 1989

Ornstein, Robert, *Multimind*, Papermac 1988

Ornstein, Robert, and Thompson, Richard, *The Amazing Brain*, Chatto & Windus, The Hogarth Press 1985

Russell, Peter, *The Brain Book*, Routledge & Kegan Paul 1979

Searle, John, *Minds, Brains and Science*, BBC 1984

Smith, Anthony, *The Mind*, Hodder & Stoughton 1984

Sternberg, Robert, *Human Abilities –
an information processing approach*,
W. H. Freeman 1985

Sternberg, Robert, *Beyond IQ*, Cambridge University Press 1985

Sternberg, Robert (ed), *Advances in the
Psychology of Human Intelligence*,
Volume 4, Lawrence Erlbaum
Associates 1988

Sternberg, Robert, and DeHerman,

Douglas (eds), *What is Intelligence?*,
Ablex Publishing Corporation 1986

Stevens, Leonard, *Explorers of the
Brain*, Angus and Robertson 1973

Taylor, David, *Mind*, Century 1983

Young, J. Z., *Philosophy and the
Brain*, Oxford University Press
1987

Young, J. Z., *Programmes of the Brain*,
Oxford University Press 1978

INDEX

MYCIN (system), 122

Napoleon Bonaparte, 26
National Union of Teachers
    (British) 67
Nature (journal), 155–6
Nestor neural net, 116–18
Netherlands *see* Holland
neurotransmitters, 71–2
neutral monism, 89
noradrenalin, 72
notational systems, 179
nutrition: and brain
    development, 79; in Japan, 158
Nyireghazi, Erwin, 59

observer-dependent effects, 16
obstetrics, 163–4
O'Connor, Neil, 62–4
Ogilvy, David, 52
optical 'neuroses', 114–16
oratory, 19
Oxfordshire Skills Programme,
    192, 194

pain, 90
Papert, Seymour, 194–7
parrots, 132
pattern-recognition, 112–14,
    116, 179
Pei, I. M., 54
Penfield, Wilder, 82
Pepperberg, Irene, 132
Petit, Ted, 77–8, 81
pets, 138
physiognomy, 80–1
Piaget, Jean, 194
pigeons, 27, 131–2
Plato, 34
PLATO package, 105
Plomin, Robert, 174

plover (bird), 28, 134–8
Popper, Sir Karl, 89
Positron Emission Tomography
    (PET) scanner, 73
Premack, David, 142
problem-solving, 108
prodigies, 48, 59, 170; *see also*
    geniuses
psychometric testing, 21–2, 45
psychophysics, 95
Putnam, Hilary, 35

quanta, 16

race: and intellectual differences,
    22, 37, 176–7
Rapid Eye Movement (REM),
    150–1
Raven's Advanced Progressive
    Matrices, 75, 160, 162–3
raw patterning ability, 179
Ray, J. J., 163–4
reaction time (RT), 67–8
Reagan, Ronald, 165
Reed, Edward, 72
Reekie, George, 118–19, 124
reflexes: trained, 29
reproductive success, 145–6
Richardson, R., 36
Riley, Douglas, 116–18
Ristau, Carolyn, 136–8
robots, intelligent, 110–14; *see
    also* artificial intelligence
Rumbaugh, Duane and Sue
    Savage, 142
Russell, Bertrand, 80
Russell, Peter, 83
Ruth, Babe, 49–50

sales patter, 17–18
Santayana, George, 20